THE COMPLETE GUIDE TO SMALL-SCALE FARMING:

Everything You Need to Know About
Raising Beef and Dairy Cattle, Rabbits,
Ducks, and Other Small Animals

REVISED 2nd Edition

By Melissa G. Nelson, D.V.M.

THE COMPLETE GUIDE TO SMALL-SCALE FARMING: EVERYTHING YOU NEED TO KNOW ABOUT RAISING BEEF AND DAIRY CATTLE, RABBITS, DUCKS, AND OTHER SMALL ANIMALS REVISED 2ND EDITION

Copyright © 2015 Atlantic Publishing Group, Inc.
1405 SW 6th Avenue • Ocala, Florida 34471 • Phone 800-814-1132 • Fax 352-622-1875
Web site: www.atlantic-pub.com • E-mail: sales@atlantic-pub.com
SAN Number: 268-1250

Library of Congress Cataloging-in-Publication Data

Nelson, Melissa G. (Melissa Gwyn), 1969- author.
  The complete guide to small-scale farming : everything you need to know about raising beef and dairy cattle, rabbits, ducks, and other small animals / author: Melissa G. Nelson, D.V.M. -- Revised 2nd edition.
     pages cm
  Includes bibliographical references.
  ISBN 978-1-62023-009-1 (alk. paper) -- ISBN 1-62023-009-7 (alk. paper) 1. Livestock. 2. Small animal culture. I. Title. II. Title: Everything you need to know about raising beef and dairy cattle, rabbits, ducks, and other small animals.
  SF61.N35 2015
  636--dc23

                         2015022823

Printed on Recycled Paper

Printed in the United States

Reduce. Reuse.
RECYCLE.

A decade ago, Atlantic Publishing signed the Green Press Initiative. These guidelines promote environmentally friendly practices, such as using recycled stock and vegetable-based inks, avoiding waste, choosing energy-efficient resources, and promoting a no-pulping policy. We now use 100-percent recycled stock on all our books. The results: in one year, switching to post-consumer recycled stock saved 24 mature trees, 5,000 gallons of water, the equivalent of the total energy used for one home in a year, and the equivalent of the greenhouse gases from one car driven for a year.

Over the years, we have adopted a number of dogs from rescues and shelters. First there was Bear and after he passed, Ginger and Scout. Now, we have Kira, another rescue. They have brought immense joy and love not just into our lives, but into the lives of all who met them.

We want you to know a portion of the profits of this book will be donated in Bear, Ginger and Scout's memory to local animal shelters, parks, conservation organizations, and other individuals and nonprofit organizations in need of assistance.

– Douglas & Sherri Brown,
President & Vice-President of Atlantic Publishing

TRADEMARK DISCLAIMER

ACKNOWLEDGMENTS

Writing a book is usually considered a lonely process, as the writer spends much time alone researching material and writing text. But no writer is an island, and during the creative process many people contribute to make a book successful. First, I'd like to thank those friends and family who supported and encouraged my decision to strike out in writing. Particularily, I'd like to thank Karen Hipple-Perez, who always had a ready ear to listen to my ideas and to help sort through things; Jennifer Hipple, a fellow writer; my sister, Rosanna Callahan; and my brother, Terry Nelson.

I would also like to thank the participants in my case studies who really made the book with their real life experiences. They were all very open and willing to share their experiences.

DEDICATION

To my parents, Henry and Suzanne Nelson, who instilled in me a healthy respect and love of all creatures great and small.

TABLE OF CONTENTS

INTRODUCTION

Farming is one of the oldest professions. Planting crops and raising livestock has been part of every culture from ancient times up to the present day. Even though very few people raise livestock or plant crops, every person is affected by agriculture. While modern day agricultural policies have made small-scale commodity crop raising (soybeans, wheat, and corn) cost prohibitive, many small-scale livestock farms thrive as a viable source of side income or family food source with a minimal outlay of cash. Livestock ownership has been closely related to individual wealth and societal advancement. Farm animals have also been mentioned frequently in literature and art: Shepherds are prominent figures in the Bible, and Egyptian carvings depict oxen pulling plows.

Kings and royalty throughout history have laid claim to large tracts of land worked by servants, slaves, and serfs. American plantation owners did the same in the United States, and large bonanza farms grew wheat and cattle in the Great Plains. Today, most chickens, turkeys, and pigs are grown by or under contract to multinational corporations in confinement buildings. Large dairies comprising thousands of cows have rapidly replaced the small dairy farms of yesteryear. Most beef cattle are fed up to slaughter weight in huge commercial feedlots.

Throughout history, most of the world's population engaged in farming; there have always been small farmers who claimed a plot of land and planted crops. If they had the means, they would also keep livestock. The bounty from the farm would primarily be used for family consumption with small amounts left over to trade or sell for items the family could not produce on the farm. This way of farming has been the backbone of American agriculture up until the end of World War II. Since then, the landscape of farming changed dramatically. The Green Revolution, the introduction of chemical fertilizers, pesticides, and herbicides, and powerful machinery capable of tilling hundreds of acres in a day prompted the demise of the small-family farm and ushered in the era of big farms. One person now did the work formerly done by 20 farmers.

This change brought with it an exodus of people from the farms and the rural communities that served them. For the past few decades, many towns and villages in rural America have become virtual ghost towns. Young adults have flocked to the larger cities where well-paying jobs are less physically intense and more pleasant than mucking out a pig stall or stacking hay in hot weather. The health benefits, working conditions, and steady paycheck offer more than the uncertainty surrounding farming. Larger farms produced surpluses of grain and livestock, lowering the grocery bill for the average consumer. This savings created a larger disposable income — or so the thought went.

There have always been stalwart small-scale farmers. They have hovered on the edges of the march of modernization, at times vilified as roadblocks on the way to progress or as environmental zealots. There was no room allowed for these backward-thinking people at the modern agriculture feed trough. However, the tide is changing, creating a paradigm shift from the thought that the top food priorities should be a cheap food supply and it should be available in large quantities. While we always will want plenty of food, people are taking a closer look at the true cost of our "cheap" food. Transporting food hundreds of miles from where it is produced is looked upon as a waste of costly fuel. Blanketing millions of acres of crops with expensive pesticides and chemical fertilizers has raised the issue of contaminated land and water. Raising livestock from hatching or birth until slaughter day in total confinement raises questions surrounding animal welfare. Losing the collective knowledge of how food is produced — no, milk is not made in the grocery store — has left the last few generations clueless on how to plant a garden, much less how to raise a chicken.

People are trickling back to the country, returning to their roots, or establishing new roots in the land. Many are former professionals who are tired of the corporate battles. Others have become fed up with the hassles of city living. Still others come seeking a healthier way of raising their children. Whatever the reason, these folks are creating a ripple in the rural landscape, reviving communities and reshaping agriculture. Optimists say this ripple may turn into a wave and could make small-scale sustainable agriculture the norm. While this may not happen, there is change happening as attested by the fact that universities and colleges are undertaking serious research in the sustainable agriculture field. Markets are opening, and merchants are anxious for milk, eggs, and meat produced using these practices.

The U.S. Department of Agriculture defines a farm as "any operation that sells at least $1,000 of agricultural commodities, or that would have sold that amount of produce (livestock) under normal circumstances," according to its Web site, **www.ers.usda. gov/data/farmincome/Sizedefinition.htm**. Many small-scale farms can easily sell that amount of livestock or produce each year, so they are counted as a farm in official numbers. Regardless if you do meet the official definition of a farm, a few factors have remained constant in agriculture throughout the years. It is a tough business requiring physical labor, while working in a field of uncertainties due to weather, disease, and injuries. Market volatility is also a big uncertainty in agriculture. All these factors can combine in a disastrous way to drive a well-meaning farmer from their livelihood, or they can build a person's character and resourcefulness in ways never thought possible.

This book will help you get off on the right foot in establishing a small-scale enterprise. You will learn how to prepare for newly hatched chickens, ducks, geese, turkeys, quails, guinea fowl, and pheasants. You will learn how to choose healthy goats, sheep, cattle, and pigs before you bring them home to your farm. Once you have your livestock, you will learn how to recognize the signs of an ill animal or bird and how to treat a sick animal. In order to properly use your investment, you will learn how to harvest milk, handle eggs, breed birds and animals, market your livestock, and butcher your own meat. In a nutshell, you will learn the ins and outs of livestock farming from experts and pros in the business. But as with most things, you will learn best by doing. Most likely, you will experience a few setbacks your first year or two. With practice, research, and determination, your foray into small-scale farming will be a fun and rewarding experience for you and your family.

Before you embark on a small-scale enterprise, do your research. Research the breeds available, the equipment needed, the physical labor requirements, and — equally important — the markets available to sell the products your livestock produce. You will have to ask yourself some tough questions. To begin, do you have the resources to finance a poultry or livestock enterprise? Can you physically handle the species you would like to raise? Is there a reliable source of feed near your farm? Is there an available, nearby market for your product, or do you have to create a market? This book can help answer these questions and more. These are just a few of the many questions you need to seriously contemplate before you make a single purchase related to small-scale farming. Instead of jumping into a larger-scale poultry or livestock operation, you might want to start with a small flock of chickens or a pair of breeding rabbits to make sure you enjoy working with animals or birds daily. Do not invest a lot of money until you are absolutely certain this is something you

would like to do as a business or to provide your family with
milk or meat.

However, do not let these precautions dissuade you from attempting to raise poultry or livestock on your farm. As long as
you go in clear-eyed and levelheaded with reasonable expectations, you just might find raising a few birds, rabbits, sheep, or
cows will suit you just fine. As you will see from some of the case
studies in this book, farming is a family affair, and children can
become just as invested as adults in rearing animals.

CHAPTER 1

Down on the Farm

Webster's Dictionary defines livestock as "animals kept or raised for use or pleasure; especially farm animals kept for use and profit." This includes common farm animals such as poultry, rabbits, sheep, goats, pigs, and cattle. If you are considering raising livestock to provide food for your family or to supplement an off-farm income, there are some issues to consider before purchasing any animals.

You will need to have some land to raise your livestock. Although a small flock of chickens, or a few ducks or geese, can easily be raised on a small lot, with larger animals you will need land to provide pasture for food, exercise, and manure disposal. Even with poultry, if you choose to let them roam outside an enclosed shelter during good weather, they will tend to forage a fair distance away from the shelter for food.

If you already own some acreage, you will want to determine if your land is zoned for agricultural use. Land that is surrounded by crop fields and other livestock farm most likely is zoned for agriculture, but if you are near a body of water or close to a town or city, you will want to check with the county or parish zoning office to make certain. Some land, while zoned for agriculture, might restrict the number of animals permitted, especially if you are near houses or a body of water. If this is the case, you might encounter the term "animal unit equivalent" (AUE). This measurement is defined as a 1,000-pound animal (the average weight of a mature beef cow) and is used to determine stocking densities of feedlots and pastures. It helps to estimate the amount of pasture forage an animal will consume and the amount of manure produced per animal. From the table below, you can see that five sheep or goats can use the same amount of pasture as one beef cow.

Animal	Weight (in pounds)	Animal Unit Equivalent (AUE)
Beef cow	1,000	1.0
Dairy cow	1,200	1.3
Bull	<2,000	1.5
Young cattle	800	.75
Sheep/goats	120	.2

All pastureland is not equal in nutritional value. Generally, the more average rainfall a given locality receives per year, the more forage produced per acre. In the United States the Great Plains region will support fewer animals per acre than an acre in the Midwest. If you are unfamiliar with the particular environment of your region, the local county extension agent can help you determine your land's pasture potential.

Another consideration is to determine if you should purchase land or rent land. Agricultural land, including pastureland, can be expensive; prices generally influence the purchase price of farmland, which can range from under $1,000 an acre up to $5,000 an acre. (The region of the country influences the price along with competition from crop farmers for land, and a real estate agent can help you determine the price of an average acre of land.) Small-scale farmers can generally get away with purchasing small tracts of land (10 to 40 acres). If you plan on renting your land, you can expect to pay from $80 an acre to more than $200 per acre, where region, competition, and productivity influence the rental price. If you do find a rent that agrees with your pocketbook, entering into a long-term contract with the landlord will help even out any future fluctuations in rent.

Outside help

Once you have settled on the land, you need to determine if you and your family have the time to devote to properly care for livestock. Each species has its own particular needs regarding housing, feeding, and general care. Smaller and young livestock will need shelter from predators and poor weather, while more mature and larger animals will be able to stand poor weather and protect themselves. It is difficult to give a particular amount of time needed to care for your animals, but generally plan to commit 10 hours a week to direct and indirect care of your animal(s). This includes building shelters, pens, and fences; maintaining buildings, equipment, and fences; feeding and watering; collecting eggs or milking the animals; cleaning pens and disposing of manure; procuring feed, hay, and bedding; plus the numerous small chores that crop up. If you have dairy animals, you will probably spend more than 10 hours a week on dairy chores, including cleaning equipment before and after milking, and with handling the milk itself.

You may need to hire outside help to assist you in some chores. If you do not have a tractor or farm equipment — tractors can cost anywhere from $5,000 for a used, small tractor in good shape upward to more than $80,000 for a new utility-type tractor — you may need to hire a tractor along with a person to operate it. While it is hard to place a price on how much will be charged for doing daily farm chores (manure spreading, skid steer operation to clean pens and buildings of manure, plowing fields, mowing hay fields, and baling hay), you should expect to pay from $30 to $60 an hour.

Many machine rental businesses will be able to rent small tractors, which can pull small plows or other machinery used for planting pastureland or small fields of crops. Skid steers can also be rented. These machines are extremely versatile and come with many bucket attachments. Hay bale spears can be used on skid steers to move the large rectangle or round hay bales. Attachments are also available to help drill holes for fence posts. Skid steers do not have the capability of doing fieldwork such as pulling a plow or a planter.

One invaluable machine to have on a small-scale farm is an all-terrain vehicle (ATV). A mid-sized new ATV can be purchased for around $6,000 and is a good first-machine investment for a small-scale farm. ATVs, depending on size, can be used to pull a harrow to break up manure pats in the pasture or to smooth a recently plowed field. They can pull trailers and small manure spreaders. Front-end attachments are available to enable you to plow snow with an ATV. Driving one around the fence line can save you time when checking pasture fences.

You may need additional help for other labor-intensive chores, such as daily milking or fencing fields. A neighboring farmer's teenaged children or a retired farmer may be looking for some part-time work. Some towns may have a local community service to help employees and employers find each other. You can also place an ad in the local newspaper or farm paper. Other farmer gathering spots, such as the local café, a farm-implement dealership, a livestock auction barn, or veterinary office, may have a bulletin board where you can post a Help Wanted ad.

Keeping your costs down

Another farm management consideration is the direct expenses involved with your livestock. The initial investment in your livestock is usually surpassed by feed costs, which includes pasture rent or cost and forage expenses. In fact, feed costs are generally the most expensive part of keeping farm animals. It is one expense that you can exercise a lot of control over and will want to keep a close eye on. Skimping on feed can lead to poor health, decreased growth, and even death. Paying too much for feed can cause your profit to disappear. Larger livestock or bigger herds can literally eat you out of house and home if feed costs are not contained.

To help keep feed costs under control, there are some general practices you can follow. On a farm, wildlife will be constantly competing with your animals for food. To avoid feeding the local raccoon population, feed should be stored in a secure room in a barn or shed with a secure door. At the very least, a metal garbage can with lid can be used to store feed. Use a rubber tie-down for extra protection against these nimble thieves. In addition to keeping your feed supply for your own animals, this will keep insects, wildlife, and birds from contaminating your feed with feces. All these creatures can spread disease to your birds and livestock. Some of the diseases can wipe out an entire flock of birds or herd of animals.

Hay should be stored off the dirt and covered to minimize wasting the outer layers of the hay bale due to spoilage from moisture. The wet layers quickly lose nutritional value and are usually unpalatable to animals. Before covering or placing hay in a building, make sure it is dry. Damp hay stacked in an enclosed shelter can heat to a high enough temperature that could cause a fire. It can also provide an ideal environment for mold to grow. Moldy hay is unpalatable to animals, and some types of mold can even be harmful, especially to pregnant or young animals.

During cold weather, feed intake — especially energy in the form of grain — for your animals will increase. If you can, provide your animal with some type of shelter from the wind. For larger, adult, non-milking livestock, a simple windbreak type of shelter will provide sufficient cover, even during the worst winter weather. A windbreaker can be any structure protecting against the prevailing wind. This can be a building, a shelterbelt of trees and shrubs planted around a pen or feedlot, or a solid fence (made of wood or metal) that the animals can stand near. Young livestock will need, at the very least, a three-sided shelter with a roof during inclement weather. Poultry will need a fully enclosed shelter even during the summer for protection from predators.

A secure fencing system will keep your livestock in and decrease your liability for accidents your animals cause. The saying "good fences make good neighbors" is still valid today. Livestock can cause a lot of damage to lawns, landscaping, and crop fields. In addition, many animals will gorge on grain or rapidly growing corn, wheat, or soybeans. This can lead to severe health problems and, frequently, death.

There are only a few states with open-range laws in which all land, both public and private (unless it is within city limits), can be foraged by livestock. The landowner has the responsibility of keeping livestock off their land. The owner of the livestock is not liable for any damages caused by the livestock, so motorists need to watch out for cattle or livestock on the road. Because of these dangers, most states do not have open range laws. They require animal owners to contain their livestock; if a stray causes a motor-vehicle accident or damage to private property, the farmer will be held responsible. Fencing requirements vary according to animals. A few strands of electrified wire will contain well-trained adult cattle. Goats need more foolproof fencing due to their inquisitive natures.

Each species will have some specific requirements to allow them to mature into healthy adults or to reach the age when they can be slaughtered. Ruminants, such as sheep, goats, and cattle, have very different digestive systems than monogastric (simple stomach) animals like pigs and humans. A ruminant's stomach is formed into three or four specialized compartments in order to be able to digest fibrous plants. Because of this, they have specific dietary requirements that vary among the ruminant animals.

When you purchase poultry and livestock, you will want to quarantine them for one to two weeks from your other animals on the farm. Even if an animal or bird appears to be healthy, they may be harboring viruses or bacteria, which takes a few days for signs of sickness to show. By isolating new arrivals, you will give a potential disease a chance to develop and run its course. Always take care of your established animals before taking care of your new ones in isolation. It is a good idea to clean manure off your boots and even dip them in disinfectant after caring for the new animals.

A good habit to develop is to practice great sanitation. Clean feeding and watering equipment immediately when you see that they are soiled by manure. Keep pens and corrals free from manure buildup and dispose of manure properly by composting or spreading onto fields for fertilizer. Depending on pen size and number of animals per pen, you may have to clean the pen daily, or you may get by with only having to clean weekly.

Disinfect equipment with bleach or commercial sanitizer between batches of flock or between uses for different animals. During insect season, manure removal, draining of stagnant water, and spraying premises with insecticides will cut down on the insect population. Flies and ticks are known carriers of disease. These simple and inexpensive measures are very effective on cutting down on disease transmission.

When you purchase young animals or poultry, remember that their immune systems are not fully developed, and they will be very susceptible to diseases — even disease that would not cause illness in adult animals. Sanitation is very important for young animals and birds. Many diseases enter the body through the mouth. Anything that contacts the mouth or that can be touched with the young animal's mouth should be cleaned and disinfected. Try to stick to a feeding schedule so as not to upset their digestive tracts, and feed the best quality feed or milk that your budget can afford.

The Pitfalls and Benefits of Raising Livestock

As with all project or jobs, rabbit rearing or pasturing a few head of cattle or sheep does have its drawbacks. A major dilemma will be how to handle the manure produced by your hay- and grain-munching critters. An average-size dairy cow can produce more than 100 pounds of manure a day that attracts flies and other insects, which can quickly become a problem if the manure is not properly cleaned and disposed. If your animals are out on pasture and if the field is large enough, manure should not be a problem. However, when the animals are confined to small pens or inside buildings, manure can quickly build up.

Plan early on how to deal with this problem. A farming neighbor may be able to help you with the use of a manure spreader, or a nearby crop farmer may let you spread the manure on his or her harvested fields. Manure can be a valuable fertilizer if properly aged or composted, but fresh manure will kill or "burn" plants. If you have just a little manure to dispose of, gardeners in your area may be eager to use the droppings for their plots.

Stables, buildings, and pens can become breeding areas for flies and insects. They are a nuisance with biting and buzzing, but most significantly, they can be a source of disease. Proper manure disposal, not letting stagnant water collect in puddles or containers, and prudent use of insecticides can help you control insects on and around your animals. Regardless of the species of livestock you raise, you will need a sturdy building or, at the very least, a secure pen to protect your animals from poor weather and keep them close to your house on occasion. All buildings and pens housing animals need to be strong and well-maintained. Protruding nails, broken boards, and snapped wires can hurt your animals or you, leading to costly medical bills. Slippery spots or holes can twist an ankle or break a bone.

Spilt grain or feed can attract wildlife to your barn or stable. Raccoons are notorious for scrounging around feed bunks or feed storage areas for a free meal. Skunks are also always on the lookout for easy to obtain feed. Both of these animals can carry the rabies virus (along with other disease) and can spread this fatal disease to livestock. Grain and feed should be stored in a critter-proof room or container. A simple garbage can with a secured lid works well for small quantities of feed.

While these negatives are bothersome, they are far outweighed by the benefits of raising livestock. Livestock eat weeds and grasses, which help keep your acreage well-mown and productive. Instead of investing thousands of dollars in a brush mower or using valuable time to run these machines, properly managed grazing livestock can maintain the grass growing between orchard trees or in pastureland.

Raising livestock can also be a fun family activity, especially if you decide to show your animals at the local fair or livestock show. As long as children are properly supervised — and when the animals become used to children — many of the chores associated with farm animal care can be given to children. The main benefit to raising livestock is that they can become a consistent source of food and side income. Who knows: Maybe your small-scale livestock farm may become a full-time occupation. It all starts with these small steps: deciding if small-scale farming will work for you and having the tools to make important decisions.

Tips for New Livestock Owners

When you purchase your first animals, ask the original owner what feed your new animal(s) are eating. Abruptly changing feed can lead to upset stomachs or worse, so try to purchase a bag of the same feed the animal is eating. Gradually switch over to any new feeds by mixing old feed with the new over a period of five to seven days. You should also request a written document listing past illnesses and a vaccination history of the animal from the current owner.

Clear the pens, buildings, and pasture you will be using for your new animals of any clutter, debris, or garbage. Most livestock breeds are fairly curious about items and may lick or try to eat items that may be toxic. Keep new arrivals separate from current farm animals for at least a week in order to acclimate the new arrival to the farm and to make sure the new animal is healthy. Gradually introduce the new animal to its new companions, preferably keeping a sturdy pen or fence between the animals. This will also minimize the change of your current animals from catching any disease the new arrival might be harboring.

Take time to familiarize yourself with your new animal's temperament and try to establish a routine. Most farm animals thrive on routine and come to expect to be fed, water, or groomed at a certain time.

CHAPTER 2

Starting Small
with Chickens

Down stage: The first few weeks of life when the chick is covered in down.

Egg bound: When the female's reproductive tract is blocked and the egg cannot pass from the body.

Evisceration: To remove the internal organs of a chicken being butchered.

Flighty: The tendency of some breeds of chickens to be excitable and nervous.

Molt: An annual process in which the chicken loses its feathers and replaces them with new feathers.

Roaster: An older chicken about 3 months to 5 months old, weighing about 5 to 7 pounds and yielding more meat per pound than a broiler or fryer.

Wattles: The fleshy tissue under the throat of some chicken breeds.

Chickens are arguably the most farm-friendly livestock the entire family can enjoy. The start-up costs and overall expenses of a small flock of chickens are the lowest of all livestock species and the quickest to turn around from newly hatched chick to market-ready. Whether you have a trio of hens to provide your family with fresh eggs or a barn full of broilers for meat, the chicken is a fun, profitable first step to starting your journey into farming.

The modern chicken has its roots in the jungle of Southeast Asia. Though Charles Darwin thought all chickens descended from the red jungle fowl, it is now known that the gray jungle fowl also contributed to the gene pool of the domestic chicken. From the breeding of these two wild fowl, we now have hundreds of breeds, types, and strains of chickens. Scientists are not in agreement as to when the chicken was first domesticated. Thailand may hold the distinction of first domesticating the chicken, but many believe there may have been multiple areas in Southeast Asia and India where wild jungle fowl were captured and kept for egg production. The earliest archeological evidence of domestication has been found in China dating back to the 5400 BC. The red jungle fowl gave us the white-skinned chicken, while the gray jungle fowl gave us a yellow-skinned chicken. Carotenoids — a natural, fat-soluble pigment found in the chickens' feed — actually form the yellow pigment in their skin. An enzyme coded by genes breaks down the carotenoids and releases vitamin A. Chickens with this gene that eat high levels of carotenoids develop yellow skin and legs.

The scientific name for the domestic chicken is *Gallus domesticus*. They come in different types: show or ornamental breeds, bantams (small, mature chicken), layers, meat-type, and dual-purpose. Which type you chose for your farm depends upon your ultimate purpose for raising chickens. The show, ornamental, and bantams are primarily raised for breeding and showing at fairs and competitions. Layers are specially bred to be prolific egg layers but are skimpy meat producers. Meat-type birds have been bred to gain weight quickly on the least amount of feed, but the hens cannot be expected to produce a large quantity of eggs. However, the eggs from a meat-type hen are perfectly fine to eat. The dual-purpose breeds are multi-purposed, combining the qualities of a meat-type and layer bird. However, they do not gain weight as quickly as meat-type birds, nor do they lay eggs as heavily as the layer breeds. Many small-scale farmers rely on these dual-purpose chickens to supply their family and customers needs.

Until commercial-sized chicken farms took over chicken production in the 1940s, most chickens were dual-purpose types and laid brown eggs. Commercial farms then started breeding layers for white eggs and meat-production birds. The dual-purpose breeds found in the United States are primarily of the American class: Barred Plymouth Rocks, White Plymouth Rocks, Rhode Island Reds, New Hampshire, and Wyandotte. Commercial layers are primarily the result of a cross between the White Leghorn and Rhode Island Red chickens. Commercial broilers are crosses between the Cornish and White Rock breeds. A small-scale chicken raiser usually will enjoy raising a dual-purpose breed.

Before you decide to raise chickens, there are a few points to take into consideration. You will need to decide what the primary purpose your chickens will serve. Do you want a fresh supply of eggs for your family? If so, keep in mind an average hen will lay 260 eggs a year — averaging five per week — for one to two years. Do you want to raise eggs to sell to the public? Then you will need to do some market research on your potential customer's needs and the demand for farm fresh eggs in your area. To find out if there is a demand for eggs, begin by approaching your friends, acquaintances, or neighbors to see if they are interested in purchasing eggs on a consistent basis. If you want to expand beyond selling a few dozen eggs a week, a local farmers' market or the local grocery store may also be interested in purchasing your eggs.

As an estimate, six hens should adequately supply enough eggs for eating and baking for a family of four. Egg production will drop a little in the winter months, as egg production is related to the length of daylight. A chicken relies upon a certain amount of daily light (approximately 14 hours) to stimulate its reproductive system. If you want to try to keep egg production up during the winter months, keep the hens in an insulated building with a light burning during the evening to add a few extra hours of light.

Do you primarily want meat? A broiler will be able to be butchered at around 6 to 8 weeks old, yielding 4 to 5 pounds of chicken. Will you have the freezer space to store your butchered chickens? Do you plan on performing the butchering process yourself, or is there a nearby butcher shop that will butcher small batches of chickens? These few questions will just be the beginning of the questions to be answered when deciding to establish a flock of chicken, even on the small scale. By reading the rest of this chapter, doing your own research, and evaluating your needs, you will be able to decide if chicken raising is for you and start this fun project with reasonable expectations.

Chicken Breeds

There are hundreds of breeds of chickens to choose from to start your flock. When you are choosing which breed to raise, keep in mind your primary purpose for raising chickens. If your plans include breeding the chickens, chose a pure breed over a hybrid breed. A hybrid breed is a cross between pure breeds, which usually results in a slightly more hardy and vigorous bird. Chicks resulting from hybrid chickens usually will not be like their parents in terms of expected egg or meat yields. They also will not look like either parent.

To get you started on choosing your breed, here is a small sampling of the more common breeds raised in small flocks in the United States. If you want a variety of chickens, you can have success with raising multiple species of chickens, provided they are raised together as newly hatched chicks. Sometimes, the chickens will appear to forage and roost near chickens of their same breed. This is mostly due to similarity in size and temperament.

Ancona: Originated near Ancona, Italy. This breed is black with white-tipped feathers. They are a smaller type of chicken that lay small, white eggs, generally around five per week. This breed can be flighty. This trait combined with their darker color helps them to avoid predators.

Andalusian: This breed had its start in Spain and was further developed in the United States and England. The Andalusian lays white eggs. Colors seen in the breed are blue (which is the required color to show this breed of chickens), black, white, or black and white. The adult blue chickens will have slate blue feathers with a narrow ridge of dark blue. This breed is an active forager, keeping feed costs down during warm weather when the chicken can remain outside. However, the bird is so active that it can run very fast, making capturing quite the event.

Australorp: The Australorp is a black chicken, which is a pro-lific brown egg layer. It was developed in Australia using Black Orpington birds. It is a good dual-purpose breed. This breed is considerably calmer than other breeds and is a heavy bird with roosters weighing around 8 pounds when mature.

Cochin: This Chinese ornamental breed is a favorite for poultry shows. They have feathered feet and come in a variety of colors. It is a very heavy breed, with roosters weighing up to 11 pounds. The hen only lays medium-sized, brown eggs for a short period of time, but makes an excellent mother. She will even become a foster mother to chicks of other breeds.

Cornish: The Cornish chicken has contributed the most to the de-velopment of the broiler industry. It is a heavy meat bird devel-oped in England. They are poor egg layers, laying only one egg a week. Color varieties are white, laced red, and dark. Cornish chickens are crossed with Plymouth Rocks to give a commercial strain (Cornish-Rock) of meat-production bird. Because of a fast growth rate, they have been known to develop crippling leg de-formities and cardiac problems.

Delaware: This breed, colored white with black points, was de-veloped in the 1940s in the United States. It is a heavy, dual-pur-pose chicken laying extra-large, brown eggs. It is also an excellent meat bird, with the males weighing close to 9 pounds at maturity. The Delaware is a great forager and has a calm disposition.

Leghorn: The Leghorn has contributed to the development of most egg-laying strains of chickens. The white Leghorn lays a lot of large, white eggs. The other varieties are not as prolific at laying eggs but still lay sizable numbers. They are very light birds, only weighing around four pounds when mature. They are very shy around humans and are flighty. They are good foragers.

New Hampshire Red: This is a dual-purpose breed, which makes a good meat bird. It also lays brown eggs and has beautiful red-brown feathers. The males weigh around 9 pounds when mature. The hens will grow broody, and they make good mothers. They are active foragers and are aggressive.

Orpington: The Orpington is a heavy, dual-purpose breed developed in England. The roosters can weigh 10 pounds when mature. The color varieties are black, blue, buff, and white. They have heavy feathering, which makes them a good choice for harsher winter climates. Their eggs are brown. This breed is very gentle and calm, which makes it a good choice for families with small children who want to be active in raising chickens. The hen can go broody if the eggs are allowed to collect in a nest.

Plymouth Rock: This dual-purpose breed was developed in the 19th century in the United States. The barred variety is the most popular, having a black and white feathering pattern. The White Plymouth Rock contributes to commercial broiler strains. They are excellent egg layers, with large, brown eggs. The breed is generally fairly docile, but some birds can become aggressive. Mature roosters generally weigh 9 ½ pounds.

Rhode Island Red: The Rhode Island Red is a dual-purpose breed. They lay very large brown eggs and are a heavy meat bird. This chicken is a good forager and is fairly docile. A mature Rhode Island Red rooster weighs 8 ½ pounds when mature. The hen can lay up to 300 eggs per year.

Silkie Bantam: This beautiful ornamental breed originated in China in the 1200s. It comes in many colors and has feathers, which look similar to human hair. They are calm, sweet birds that lay small to medium sized, white to brown eggs. The Silkie Bantam has blue earlobes, bones, and flesh, which are caused by melanin, a pigment normally found only in the skin. The Silkie is also unique from other chickens in that it has five toes on each foot as opposed to the four found on most breeds. Hens only lay about three eggs a week, but they will sit on eggs of other chickens or even on other bird species eggs.

Sussex: A good dual-purpose breed developed in England. They are good egg-layers with large, light brown eggs. The feather coloring can be speckled, light, or red. The male weighs around 9 pounds when mature. They are excellent foragers and have a calm temperament. Hens lay around 250 eggs per year and can become broody.

Wyandotte: The Wyandotte is a good dual-purpose breed. They are great egg layers, laying large, brown eggs. This breed comes in many colors and feathering patterns. They are a docile, talkative breed of chicken and are a popular show breed. Wyandotte chickens are good foragers, and an adult male will weigh 8 ½ pounds when mature.

Preparing For Your Baby Chicks

Once you have decided to raise chickens, you will need to plan for your new arrivals. Chickens can be raised in almost any building, provided it is draft-free and predator-proof. Chicks still in the down stage cannot adequately insulate themselves against wind, while fully feathered chickens can fluff their feathers, creating air pockets to protect against wind and colder weather.

Predators are a big problem with all ages of chickens. Chicks need to stay inside a shelter both day and night for temperature regulation and safety. Raccoons, cats, weasels, dogs, foxes, coyotes, skunks, and prey birds all enjoy a chicken dinner. Older chickens can venture outside, provided they have an enclosed shelter to escape predators. Most savvy chicken owners will always lock their chickens in a secure shelter overnight.

Chicks, like any newborn animal, will need some special care to ensure they get off on the right foot to minimize losses. While all chickens should have fresh food and water, a chick is unable to regulate body heat while covered in down, so they need a constant source of external heat. Their immune systems are also less capable of fighting off disease, so extra attention should be paid to keeping their environment clean and reasonably sanitary.

You will want to start with purchasing your chicks from a reputable source whose top priority is hatching healthy chicks. Mail-order companies or feed stores are fine, provided they can tell you the source of their chicks. You will want to make sure the chicks were hatched in a reputable hatchery, not in a backyard with questionable sanitation standards. Hatcheries specializing in poultry are the main suppliers to feed stores or mail-order companies. Usually you can order directly from the hatchery, provided you purchase a minimum number of chickens. Another added feature to investigate is whether the hatchery participates in the National Poultry Improvement Plan (NPIP) and if the breeding flock is yearly tested and certified disease-free. The NPIP is a voluntary program between federal and state governments and the poultry industry to prevent the spread of poultry diseases.

After deciding on the breed(s) of chickens you want, you will next want to decide if you want to purchase cockerels (young males), pullets (young females), or a straight run (mix of both sexes). If you plan on butchering your chickens for meat, you will want all cockerels. Males will put on weight faster and will be heavier than females; how much weight varies depending on breed. If your plans include a laying flock, you will want to purchase pullets. You do not need a rooster in order to get eggs. A straight–run group will generally cost a little less per chick then a group segregated by sex. Most hatcheries will guarantee you will get around a 95 percent sexed group (the percent of chickens' which sex has been accurately determined), so do not be too surprised to find one of your pullets is actually a rooster when they mature.

The mail-order company will tell you when your chickens will be shipped. They will generally require you to order a minimum number of chicks to provide enough body heat for shipping, usually 25 or more chicks. Also, shipping is done primarily in spring and early summer to take advantage of the more temperate weather. Be sure to have someone available to immediately unpack the chickens and put them in their pen when they arrive at your doorstep.

If you decide to purchase your chicks from a feed store, be sure to examine the condition of their pen. If the pen, water, and feed are dirty or if there are any dead chicks in the pen, do not purchase your chickens from that store. The chicks' health might already be compromised from a poor start in life. It is also important to check the vent (anus) of the chicks. If there is any fecal build-up, the chicks might be harboring a disease.

Setting up the pen

Prior to bringing the chicks home, you should have the pen set up and ready. You will need the following equipment before the chicks arrive:

- Heat lamp

- Electricity source

- Heat bulb

- Waterer

- Feeder

- Means to enclose the chicks near the water, feed, and light

- Shavings or sawdust for bedding

Heat lamps and bulbs can be purchased at farm supply stores or hardware stores. Waterers should be 1 gallon or less and should be slightly elevated after the first few days to prevent build-up of shavings and manure from the chick's natural tendency to scratch and kick bedding into the water or feed trough. Likewise, feeders should be raised slightly after a few days. You should provide one waterer per 25 chicks, and 1 inch of feeder space per chick.

For the first few weeks, the chickens can be raised in a large stock tank or similar container. The main priority is that the container is cleaned, bleached, and dried before the chicks arrive. A mild bleach solution (1 teaspoon per gallon of water) or vinegar can be used to disinfect the pen, waterers, and feeders. Letting the equipment dry in the sun ensures all disease-causing germs are killed.

Spread a layer of bedding in the bottom of your container, then hang your heat lamp. Make sure that the heat lamp will not be in contact with any combustible materials and that it is securely fastened. You will need to adjust the heat lamp based upon chick behavior, so ensure that the lamp can be easily moved. Start out with hanging the lamp so the bottom is 12 inches from the bedding. A basic aluminum shade lamp found at any hardware store provides an affordable and safe heat source.

Fill the waterers with fresh water. You can add a pinch of vitamin and electrolyte solution to the water for the first week to give your chicks a good start. Fill the feeder up with chick starter, which can be purchased at farm stores or a local grain elevator. This pre-blended feed is carefully formulated to provide the chicks with a balanced blend of grain, protein, energy, vitamins, and minerals.

The medicated chick starters will have a coccidiostat, a drug added to help control coccidiosis. Nonmedicated chick starter will work as well, provided you are diligent about daily cleaning of waterers and feeders and do not overstock the pen with chickens. There is no medication that can take the place of cleanliness and good husbandry.

When your chicks arrive, take each one out of the box and dip its beak in the water. This will ensure that the chicks get a drink of water and that they will know where the water source is located. Then, release the chicks under the heat lamp. After all chicks have been released, observe them frequently over the course of the day to make sure they are all able to eat and drink. If they huddle under the lamp, the lamp should be lowered to provide more heat. If they are scattered far away from the lamp, they are probably too warm, and the lamp should be raised a few inches. This is a good general rule for most young animals.

A covering of chicken wire or other woven wire over the container — even if your building is predator-proof — will give you extra assurance that nothing will sneak into the pen and kill your investment. If you have a shallow container, it will also help contain the chicks as they get older and are testing out their ability to jump and flutter.

Incubating Eggs

If you would rather hatch your own chicks, a fun family project is to incubate eggs, either purchased or laid by the family hen. To begin, you will need an incubator, a hygrometer for measuring humidity inside the incubator, and a regular thermometer. It takes 21 days for a chick to hatch and requires close monitoring during these three weeks.

Before your eggs arrive, the incubator should warm up for one week. Read the instructions that come with the incubator very carefully as each manufacturer will have some specific requirements on their product. Incubators generally come in two types: a still-air incubator or a fan-forced incubator. Air temperature in the still-air incubator should read 101.5°F at the top of the eggs; a fan-forced incubator temperature should read 99.5°F. A fan-forced incubator will use a fan to evenly distribute heat throughout the incubator. A fan-forced incubator will cost more, but for small batches of eggs, a still-air incubator will give an adequate hatch. Prices for incubators range from $60 to more than $400.

In addition to temperature, the humidity inside the incubator is important to maintain. For the first 18 days of incubation, the humidity should range between 60 to 65 percent. For the remaining three days, the humidity should be increased to between 80 to 85 percent. It cannot be stressed enough to carefully monitor the temperature and humidity during the incubation period. Chicks will not hatch or will be unhealthy in an improperly maintained incubator.

If you purchase eggs, you will need to "settle" the eggs for a day to allow the air-cell inside to return to a normal size. Those swiped from a broody hen can be directly placed inside the incubator. To settle the eggs, store them with the more pointed side down at 55 to 60°F. After settling, or if they have been taken from a hen, distribute the eggs evenly throughout the incubator. You will need to turn the eggs twice a day for the first 18 days to prevent the chick from sticking to the side of the egg. After the 18th day, stop turning to let the chick orientate itself inside the shell. Increase the humidity level inside the incubator and fight the urge to open the incubator door. Opening the door will drop the temperature and humidity, and it will take a few hours for the incubator to return to the proper levels of heat and humidity, which could cause problems with the hatch.

Once the chicks start to break their shells, do not attempt to help them out of the shell. They need to do this on their own to develop the strength they need to survive the new world. If a chick cannot come out of its shell on its own, it will probably not be able to survive. Leave unhatched eggs in the incubator for two to three days after the first chick hatches. After that, remove the eggs and discard — these chicks have died. If your chicks hatch very wet and "mushy," the humidity inside the incubator was too high. Remove the moisture from the incubator if the chicks fail to fluff up their down. Once the down is fluffed, and when they are running around the incubator, transfer them to the prepared brooder area. The chicks should be ready for transfer in a few hours after hatching.

Feeding and Equipment

Photo provided by Annette and Kay Fernholz

At around 4 to 5 weeks of age, your chicks will be fully feathered out and will be large enough to move out of the brooding pen. The requirements for a chicken coop remain the same as one for chicks: safe and secure from predators, dry, and protected from heavy winds. A shed or an unused part of a building can be used to keep the chickens. Keep them confined to their new home for a few days; then, they can be let outside during the daylight hours. They will come home to roost, so to speak, when evening approaches, and they should be locked in for the night.

As the chicks grow, they will have certain requirements for floor space, feeder space, and waterer space. The minimum amount of space for a broiler of lightweight layer is 1 square foot. Heavier or larger birds will require twice that amount. Most small-scale chicken raisers will not have a problem meeting the minimum floor space requirement since the space requirement is so small. More floor space will mean less chance that disease will spread.

All birds should be able to eat and drink at the same time. This typically means you should allow 2 to 3 inches of space for each bird if you use trough feeders or waterers. If you use circular waterers or feeders, 1 to 2 inches per bird will be adequate. Trough feeders or waterers are long and rectangular-shaped plastic or metal pans. Circular feeders and waterers have a round base onto which a tall, cylinder-shaped holding pan is attached to the base. The water or feed then gradually flows into the base where the chickens feed.

Chickens also have some special lighting needs, but the artificial light does not to be elaborate or bright. In fact, too bright of a light might lead to pecking. Broilers can be placed under 24 hours of light (incandescent 40 watt bulbs) to encourage feeding; however, doing so might waste electricity, and pushing broilers for growth might lead to early death and leg deformities. A good compromise might be to provide broilers with 18 hours of light a day. At around 10 weeks of age, chickens raised as layers should be placed on short light periods of fewer than 12 hours a day. If you purchased your chicks in the spring or early summer, natural lighting will accomplish this lighting requirement. This will help them to mature properly and have optimal lifetime egg production.

Baby chicks should be fed a quality, commercially prepared starter diet. They do not need any supplemental feed at this time. In fact, giving them vegetable scraps or grass might keep them from consuming adequate quantities of starter, slowing their growth or causing death. At 6 weeks of age, the chicks should be switched to a grower ration, which is lower in protein than the starter ration. When your hens reach laying age (around 4 to 6 months old) they should be switched to a layer ration, which has high calcium content to promote good egg formation. Laying hens should also have crushed oyster shells to make sure they consume adequate amounts of calcium for proper eggshell development. They can also be provided grit (small pieces of mineral) to help digest food properly. Do not forget to provide the most important nutrient: water. Water should be available at all times and should be placed into clean waterers. The waterers should be checked on a daily basis and cleaned as soon as they become soiled with litter or feces.

Health Concerns

Behavioral problems

Pecking and cannibalism are major problems in chickens. The term "hen pecked" comes from chickens' social need for a pecking order — or social class — formed within the flock. The rest of the flock will defer to the top bird, giving him or her access to food, water, and space first. A flock of chickens will establish a social hierarchy and will coordinate flock activities such as drinking, eating, dust bathing, and roosting. Every chicken knows its rank in the order, and the rank seldom changes unless an illness or death occurs. Commercial growers will trim newborn chicks' beak to cut down on pecking and cannibalism. However, beak trimming will not allow your chickens to forage effectively. As long as you are not restrictively confining your hens to tiny, commercial-type pens, pecking and cannibalism should not be a problem.

Chickens have good eyesight and can see colored objects in bright sunlight. This will lead them to use their sensitive beaks to explore for new food. If their beaks become soiled or if they eat a mushy food, they will wipe their beaks off on the ground. Their beaks can be compared to our hands because they use the beaks to explore and carry things. An intact beak allows the chicken to fully explore their world.

If you have a particularly aggressive bird, it can be placed in a separate pen but within sight of the rest of the flock for a few days to help it calm down. It can then be reintroduced to the flock, but be sure to monitor its behavior. Placing extra feed and water sources in the pen will also cut down on competition for these resources. If one bird has been de-feathered by the other birds, there are ointments that can be placed on her feathers to deter pecking. Finally, there are plastic devices that can be placed on the beak of particularly aggressive birds, which will allow them to eat and drink but not peck.

Taming a mean rooster

Mean roosters have turned many people off from raising chickens. With their well-developed spurs, rooters can inflict serious wounds when they see you as a threat to their flock dominance. Each time you enter the coop, you will have to remind your rooster that you are the top dog of the flock by following the steps given in this section.

An alpha rooster usually dominates the pecking order of a flock by getting first dibs at food, water, and hens. The hens also have an alpha hen that is the boss. Unlike the roosters, hen social order is harder to see, but it is there. The alpha rooster asserts his dominance constantly. If another chicken attempts to eat first or another rooster tries to mate a hen, the alpha male will rush over and administer a good peck or even pummel the out-of-bounds interloper with beak, claws, and wings.

Your job is to make sure you are not the victim of such an attack. Starting when the chickens are small, take a few minutes each day to observe their behavior. When the chicks start to fight (or spar), break them apart by gently pushing them back with your fingers. Each fight you see, do the same thing. This will let the flock know that you are in charge. As they get older, you will still have to reinforce your dominance. It is fine to pick up a rooster and pet him. But a rooster should not be eager to approach you. If he does, he will think that he is the top chicken, not you. It will not hurt to take an occasional swat at him if he seems too comfortable with you.

Do not let the rooster eat before the hens. Doing so will give him the cue that he is dominant in the flock when, in reality, you should be the dominant member (in his mind) of the flock. In essence, you are top rooster and need to allow the hens to eat before him, the less-dominant rooster. If he tries to come to the feeder first, push him away so the hens eat first. After the hens are eating, it is fine if the rooster begins to eat. If a rooster tries to breed a hen in your presence, push him off and chase him away. It is the same concept as eating; he has to wait until you leave to be able to breed the hens.

The main thing to remember when it comes to roosters is that you have to be on guard at all times. If these techniques do not work, or if you are unable to be consistent in asserting your dominance, it might be safer for the rooster to be destined for the soup bowl.

Nutritional deficiencies

Nutritional deficiencies are two problems with chickens, especially while they are still growing. Rickets (vitamin D deficiency) and vitamin A deficiency are the primary nutritional disorders in chickens. Vitamin A deficiency will result in poor weight gain, poor feather formation, and death. Adult chickens deficient in vitamin A will have nasal and eye discharges, and decreased egg production. Most feeds will have plenty of vitamin A, provided the feed is fresh and has not been sitting on the shelf for a long period of time. Fresh vegetation will also provide your chickens with plenty of vitamin A.

Deficiencies of calcium and phosphorus will cause rickets (poor bone growth and formation) in chickens. In older hens, a similar deficiency will cause osteoporosis. Heavy-laying caged hens are more likely to suffer from osteoporosis, making their bones fragile and prone to easy breakage. This is caused by loss of calcium from the bones to form eggs shells. A lack of exercise also contributes to osteoporosis. A properly fortified feed, along with exercise and access to free range to plants, can help prevent rickets and osteoporosis.

Parasitic infections

Parasitic infections can plague your chickens, especially if they have access to dirt. Lice, coccidian, roundworms, and hairworms are the main parasites affecting chickens. Check your chickens daily to assess their overall health. Things to observe include feather loss, weight loss, unthrifty appearance, sitting huddled away from the flock, and decreased egg production. Heavily infected chickens can be more prone to developing other diseases that can quickly lead to death.

Most chickens raised with access to dirt flooring will harbor a few internal parasites. These generally will not cause symptoms or problems and are not easily transmitted to humans. Chickens get parasites by eating parasite eggs found on food, dirt, or water. Insects, earthworms or snails — all tasty treats to foraging chickens — also carry the parasites or eggs in their body. Coccidian, roundworms, and hairworms are common intestinal worms of chickens. To control parasites in chickens, there are some specific things you can do:

- Do not overcrowd your shed or outside pens.

- Try to keep wild birds away from your chickens.

- Use insecticides, if necessary, to control insects in sheds.

- Change bedding frequently and keep it dry.

- Remove droppings to keep chickens from pecking at them.

- Keep your chickens on a quality feed formulated with plenty of vitamins.

- If you suspect internal parasites, have your local veterinarian identify the species so you can properly medicate the birds.

Infectious diseases

Contagious diseases such as fowl cholera, fowl pox, colibacillosis, mycoplasmosis, avian influenza, and Newcastle disease can strike a flock and cause decreased growth, egg production, and death.

Colibacillosis is an infection with *Escherichia coli (E. coli)*. The signs of colibacillosis are variable. Birds can suddenly drop dead with no prior signs of disease. Other chickens have a chronic infection leading to a "poor doing" chicken. The bacteria can infect the blood, intestinal tract, or lung, which can cause diarrhea, labored breathing, and coughing. The best way to prevent colibacillosis is through sanitizing feeders and waterers on at least a weekly basis and keeping the pen and bedding clean. Providing good ventilation in the pen or coop will also help minimize the impact of this disease. Antibiotic treatment may or may not be successful due to the many strains and types of *E. coli*.

Mycoplasmosis is big problem in poultry. Different strains of this organism can cause lung disease (airsacculitis), sinus disease, or joint infection. Antibiotics can be used to control mycoplasmosis, but like most infectious disease, prevention through good sanitation and ventilation will save you from the heartache of dealing with this difficult-to-treat disease.

Fowl cholera is caused by the bacteria *Pasteurella multocida*. It is spread to chickens by free-flying birds and other mammals such as dogs, cats, raccoons, rats, mice, and opossums. Many birds in a flock may be affected, causing sudden death, diarrhea, ruffled feathers, and joint problems. Treatment will be aimed at the entire flock through antibiotics in the water. Check with your local veterinarian or extension agent on the best type of medication to use. Prevention through good rodent and wild bird control, as well as good sanitation, will help minimize the chance of an outbreak of fowl cholera in your flock.

Infectious coryza, commonly known as a cold, occurs in adolescent and adult chickens. A chicken with coryza will have swelling of the face, and nasal and eye discharge. Egg production will drop as well. Antibiotics in the water or feed can help control coryza. Prevention is aimed at keeping the organism out of the flock through making sure only healthy chickens are introduced into the flock. Purchase your chicks from a single source, and do not mix young chickens with older chickens. In fact, practicing an "all-in, all-out" management style will prevent many infectious diseases from occurring. This means the only chickens on your farm will be ones that were purchased from the same source at the same time, and new additions will only occur when all the old chickens are gone.

Newcastle disease is a viral disease that affects all bird species. Infected birds spread the virus in their droppings and through droplets from the respiratory tract. It can also be spread through dust contaminated with the virus. Depending on the viral strain, the disease can be mild, moderate, or severe. Young birds are typically affected the worse and may have facial swelling, trouble breathing, or convulsions. Vaccinations have helped to control Newcastle disease in poultry.

Avian influenza can cause a wide range of signs in poultry ranging from a mild disease with few deaths to a highly fatal, rapidly spreading disease. Waterfowl are more resistant to avian influenza than other poultry breeds. In fact, waterfowl can serve as a source of avian influenza to turkeys and chickens, causing serious disease in these two species. The signs of avian influenza are very variable depending upon the strain of virus. Signs include sneezing, coughing, ruffled feathers, depression, diarrhea, swollen head, or sudden death. There is no specific treatment or vaccination. Prevention revolves around keeping wild birds away from domestic poultry flocks.

Putting Your Investment to Work

Breeding

Before you embark on breeding your chickens, take some time to decide what your intentions are. Do you want to have replacement layers and some broilers to feed up? Are you interested in breeding purebred chickens or in breeding one of the less common breeds? Do you hope to sell baby chicks? Breeding chickens and incubating eggs will take some planning on your part to ensure your chicks are healthy and able to survive. Most hatcheries hatch out eggs for sale in the spring and early summer to coincide with favorable weather for raising chicks. This is especially important in the northern latitudes where harsh winter weather makes keeping a brooder area at the proper temperature in un-heated and poorly insulated buildings impossible. You should aim for a spring hatch.

You will be hatching out both males and females. If you breed a laying-type chicken, the males will not make the best meat birds. They can be raised for meat, although most likely at a financial loss. Meat-type female birds will not necessary be the best lay-ers, although they can be butchered for meat. Hybrid birds, as opposed to purebred strains, will not necessarily hatch out in the same likeness of the parents. So chose your breed based on your desired outcome. Cockerels reach breeding age at 17 to 19 weeks of age. One rooster can service between six to 12 hens. Hens reach breeding age at 18 to 20 weeks of age. The hens and rooster should be placed in an indoor pen with nest boxes (one box per four hens) so you can collect the eggs twice daily. The collected eggs can be stored in egg cartons at 55–60°F for up to seven days before they are incubated.

Eggs should be gently cleaned of manure and dirt before storage or placing in the incubator. They should be candled five days after being placed in the incubator. A broody hen can also sit on a nest of eggs if you do not have an incubator. She should be left alone to care for the eggs. Provide her with feed and water at all times.

Management of layers

You will need to properly manage your laying flock in order to get a consistent, quality, and clean supply of eggs. As discussed previously, laying hens will need to be fed a steady diet of laying hen feed, which has a higher calcium level than the other types of chicken feed. In addition, crushed oyster shells (which come in convenient 40- to 50-pound sacks) should be placed in a separate feeder from the feed. Keep the feeders and waterers full of feed, oyster shells, and water at all times for your hens.

You will want to make sure you can find the eggs once the hens start laying. This can be accomplished by fencing the flock in so they cannot wander off into the woods or other protected area to start a nest. Some breeds of hens are more broody than others. This means they will lay an egg daily in a hidden nest and try to sit on them to hatch out chicks. They will even do this if there is no rooster to fertilize the eggs.

Provide your hens with a nest box so they have a sheltered, shady place to lay their eggs. This need not be fancy or elaborate, but it does need to be maintained and cleaned frequently. Eggs can quickly become soiled by feces or mud, which can also stain the shell, leading to unappealing eggs. There should be one nest box for every four hens in your flock. This will help to keep the eggs clean and to minimize egg breakage. Depending on the type you purchase, the boxes should have a deep layer of litter to cushion the eggs and to absorb any waste material. Nest boxes should be placed inside a building. Rats, skunks, raccoons, and snakes will eat eggs, so the building should be predator-proof, especially at night. Hens will learn to come back to the pen to lay eggs, so they can be let out of the pen during the day to forage and exercise.

Eggs should be picked twice daily. Most chickens will lay their eggs before 10 a.m. If the temperature is below freezing, check for eggs frequently, as they will freeze. By picking eggs frequently, you will also help to minimize breakage. Hens will frequently peck at broken eggs and sometimes can develop an appetite for eggs, breaking intact eggs just to eat them. Once you have collected the eggs, they will need to be processed. The eggs should be washed as soon as possible after they have been picked. Wash water should be a little warmer than the eggs; lukewarm water will be sufficient. If the water is colder than the eggs, dirt and bacteria can be drawn into the egg through pores in the shell. Using warmer water will make the contents inside the egg swell and push the dirt away from the pores. A mild detergent can also be used to wash eggs. Use running water to clean the eggs and do not allow them to sit in water to minimize any bacterial cross contamination between the eggs.

Eggs should then been dried and cooled after washing. To properly store, they should be placed in eggs cartons with the pointy end down and the carton should be placed inside a refrigerator. Properly cleaned and stored eggs can remain safe to eat for four weeks or longer.

Candling eggs

Eggs are candled in order to see if the eggs are fertilized or not. Despite daily gathering of eggs, occasionally you may miss one for a few days, and an embryo may develop if you have a rooster running with your hens. If you plan on selling your eggs, you should candle them to make sure your customers do not crack open an egg with a chick growing inside. Eggs are also candled if you are incubating fertilized eggs to determine if the chick is growing or if it has died inside the shell.

Surprisingly, an actual candle does not have to be used to candle eggs. To candle the eggs, you will need a darkened room and a bright, direct light source. A bright flashlight or a lamp with a bright bulb can be used. You can also purchase a commercial candler through poultry supply companies. Hold the large end of the egg up to the light and slowly turn it. You should be able to see the air sac, the yolk, and the pores through the eggshell. Dark or brown eggs will make it a little harder to see through the shell. In a fertilized egg, there will be a spot — a thin red ring or blood vessels — around the yolk. If the egg has been incubated about a week, you will be able to see the embryo's eye, the shadow of its body, and it may even move.

CASE STUDY: A FARM FULL OF CHICKENS

Annette and Kathleen Fernholz
Earthrise Farm
Madison, Minnesota
www.earthrisefarmfoundation.org

Photo provided by Annette and Kay Fernholz

Earthrise Farm is a family farm located outside of Madison, Minnesota. Sisters Annette and Kathleen (Kay) Fernholz moved back to Madison 14 years ago to run their parents' farm after decades of being away. They served for 40 years with the Sisters of Notre Dame convent as educators. They still take their calling in education seriously, and their farm is a haven of learning for interns and community members who want to have a basic understanding of where their food comes from.

The Fernholz sisters decided to raise chickens as their mother had a real devotion to caring for her birds. They keep around 150 Bovan Goldline hens and follow organic standards to produce a high-quality egg, rich in omega-3 fatty acid. Their chickens run free around the homestead and eat organically raised feeds, such as buckwheat, barley, and flax that help boost the omega-3 in the eggs. They also have four acres of garden to provide the local community with fair cost of production produce through a Community Supported Agriculture (CSA) program. The rest of the 240-acre farm is farmed organically by three of their brothers.

They caution beginning farmers to keep meticulous records in order to track costs of production versus the price of eggs. Feed costs can quickly exceed the price of eggs. The Fernholz's also suggest that a chicken producer should make certain they enjoy working with chickens, as there will most likely be some years where the egg enterprise may not breakeven with cost of production. Starting with a small number of birds will go a long way to helping understand the bird and to help a beginning farmer develop a market. One way to help with markets is to join with other egg producers in the area to set a minimum price for the eggs so no one person can undercut the other.

Earthrise Farm is a busy place with chickens scratching around the grounds and workers busy with the chicken chores. The most time-consuming chores on Earthrise Farm are: collecting, cleaning, candling, and packaging the eggs, cleaning the hen houses, and distribution of eggs to CSA members and local grocery stores. They recommend a beginning organic-egg farmer have an insulated barn that is heated to 55°F in the winter to ensure egg production stays steady. Securing an affordable and nearby source of organic grain is also a necessity to the organic egg producer.

At Earthrise Farm, the Fernholz sisters are accomplishing their mission of providing the local community with nutritious, fairly priced food along with community education.

CHAPTER 3

The World
of Waterfowl

Terms To Know 🖊

Drake: A male duck. Mature drakes (except for the Muscovy breed) can be differentiated from the duck by curled tail feathers.

Duck: A female duck and the general term for the species.

Duckling: A young duck.

Gander: A male goose.

Goose: A female goose and the general term for the species.

Gosling: A young goose.

Having a flock of ducks or geese running around the farmstead is truly an amusing and heartening sight. These birds offer many benefits to the small-scale farmer providing meat, weed control, and — in the case of geese — even a natural alarm system. After the first few weeks of life, ducks and geese are fairly easy keepers and make great foragers for bugs and weeds. Ducks are related to swans and geese and all ducks, except for Muscovy ducks, were domesticated from the wild Mallard. The Chinese are credited with first domesticating the duck around 1000 BC. They herded flocks of ducks for hundreds of years to rice paddies to consume insects, snails, slugs, small reptiles and waste rice. Geese were domesticated in Greece around 1500 BC from flocks of wild geese. Most goose breeds are descended from the Graylag breed. The Chinese and African breeds of geese are descended from the Swan goose.

Ducks are much smaller than most geese. When full grown, a duck can weigh from 4–11 pounds and can live as long as 12 years. Geese are fairly large birds, weighing as much as 30 pounds when mature, and they live much longer than ducks — up to 25 years. Geese are fairly loyal family members and prefer to choose a mate for life. They are also very protective of their flock, making them great farm "watchdogs."

Ducks can provide a reliable source of eggs and meat. Like chickens, some breeds have been bred to be prolific layers of eggs, while other breeds have been developed to provide substantial quantities of meat. If you plan on collecting eggs from your waterfowl, ducks would be the best choice. Two breeds, the Indian Runner and Khaki Campbell, are best known for their prolific egg production. Geese do not lay as many eggs as ducks, but the Emden breed will lay around three-dozen eggs during the breeding season.

While the eggs of ducks and geese can be eaten as chicken eggs, geese eggs are generally not consumed due to their larger size and because geese lay so few eggs. Most likely there will not be a market for the eggs, but your family may enjoy eating them. Duck eggs have a higher yolk fat content and white protein content than chicken eggs, so when cooked, the whites do not become as stiff as chicken eggs. If the duck has been eating a lot of algae, worms, or grubs, the eggs may have a slightly musty taste. Eggs should be collected twice daily, washed in warm water, and promptly stored in the refrigerator.

Duck meat is higher in iron, niacin, and selenium than many other types of meat. Good duck meat breeds include Pekin, Rouen, Muscovy, and Aylesbury. The meat from both ducks and geese is all dark meat and is richer than chicken or turkey due to the higher fat content — this gives the meat a distinctive taste popular in many gourmet restaurants. Ethnic markets are particularly interested in obtaining a steady supply of quality duck and goose meat. Geese have provided a rich source of protein for centuries, with many people enjoying the meat and liver. But even more so, a roasted goose has long been a traditional Christmas dinner over the centuries. Foie gras is made from the fattened livers of force-fed geese and is especially common in French cultures. Geese meat breeds include the Emden, Toulouse, Chinese, and Africans.

Unlike other poultry species, domesticated waterfowl are fairly disease-resistant. However, like the very young of any animal species, ducklings and goslings need to be kept dry and warm when they are covered in down. Once the young are fully feathered, they thrive on being outdoors in all but the coldest of weather. They do keep a layer of down under their feathers, which insulates them from cold. In addition, they have an oil gland at the base of the tail. They will rub their chins and cheeks over the gland, collecting the oil, which it will then rub onto its feathers. This oil makes their outer feathers waterproof. Mothers will rub some of the oil from her oil gland onto the down of her young until they are able to perform this function on their own. Ducks and geese need to keep their feathers in tip-top condition to keep them dry and warm, and they spend a substantial amount of time preening.

Geese will need shelter during subzero weather and protection from aggressive predators like coyotes. Ducks and geese will also need shade during hot weather. Ducks should be brought into a shelter every night, as smaller predators like raccoons, foxes, and weasels can decimate a flock in a few hours. Geese naturally flock together and will return to a home base each night, even when they wander more than a mile away from home. Vehicles also can take their toll on a flock, so if you plan to keep waterfowl, they will need to be kept away from roadways.

Duck Breeds

When deciding on which breed of duck you would like to raise, there are two main types to consider. Ornamental ducks are ducks kept for the pleasure of keeping waterfowl. Their striking plumage and amusing behavior are their primary benefit to humans, and generally they do not make good meat or egg producers. Utility, or commercial ducks, have been bred for meat, down, or egg production. This is the primary type of duck breeds discussed in this chapter. Ducks come in many different feather colors, and males and females can be distinguished by feather color.

Indian Runner: This breed of duck is unique in its upright stance, looking like a bowling pin on webbed feet. It was developed from the wild mallard in the East Indies two centuries ago. Because of their physical conformation, they run rather than waddle like the typical duck, making walking to the fields an easy task. They are very active foragers, especially of insects, snails, and slugs, and put on a good deal of flesh, considering they are a lighter duck. Indian Runners are great egg layers, sometimes even outlaying chickens. Generally, females lay around 200 eggs each year. They are not considered good egg sitters, so eggs from a female Indian Runner may need to be incubated by another hen or in an incubator. The adult male Indian Runner seldom weighs more than 5 pounds.

Khaki Campbell: The Khaki Campbell is a breed developed in England by Adele Campbell in the late 1800s. Campbell crossed her Indian Runner hen with a Rouen Drake in order to produce ducks that would lay well and have bigger, meatier bodies. Her breeding strategy worked because the resulting breed, the Khaki Campbell, is an excellent layer. The hens will more readily sit on the eggs, unlike the Indian Runner duck. A hen will lay more than 300 eggs a year. The Khaki Campbell does have a flighty temperament and needs room to forage. They are also adaptable to variable climates, performing well in hot, dry deserts; wet, tropical environments; or in cold, winter weather. As an added bonus to their eggs, the Khaki Campbell is a prolific insect, slug, and algae eater.

Pekin duck

Pekin: The Pekin is the most common breed of domestic duck. These white ducks are great for meat production, as they grow rapidly and pack on more pounds of meat per pound of feed than other ducks. The Pekin duck was developed in China from ducks residing in the canals of Nanjing. An adult female will lay around 200 eggs a year. They are not as broody as other ducks so they may not sit on a nest. Drakes can weigh more than 12 pounds and females more than 11 pounds.

Rouen: The Rouen breed is very similar in coloring to the wild Mallard. They were originally developed in France and were imported to England, where the breed was bred into the modern-day Rouen. There are two types of Rouen: the production and the standard. The production Rouen weighs between 6 and 8 pounds; the standard Rouen is much larger, weighing between 8 and 10 pounds. Females lay about 70 greenish eggs a year. They are good meat producers, but take from 6–8 months to mature. This slow maturation rate has led to commercial duck growers' reluctance to raise Rouens on a large scale for the meat market. The meat from the Rouen is leaner than the Pekin, making it a popular duck for restaurants.

Muscovy: The Muscovy is unique in that it was not developed from Mallards. It is a Brazilian breed that can become quite large; males can weigh in at more than 10 pounds. They come in a variety of colors, but they all have a distinctive bright red tissue above the beak and around the eyes. They do not swim much, as they have underdeveloped oil glands — which makes their feathers less water-resistant than other breeds — but they do have sharp claws, which they use to roost in tree branches. The females become broody three times a year and will incubate the eggs of other ducks or poultry species.

Cayuga: This breed was developed in New York in the 1800s from native ducks. They are considered to be a medium-weight duck and are primarily used as a meat bird. Adult males reach 8 pounds. They have unique coloring, with a greenish-blue sheen over dark feathers. Eggs from the Cayuga can be variable colors, depending on the season. When they first start laying eggs, the eggs may have a gray or black color. As the laying season progresses, the eggs will start to lose this dark coloring and may even become white.

Geese Breeds

White goose

Emden: The Emden was developed in Germany and the Netherlands and is the most common commercial goose breed. They are typically white with orange bills and feet and blue eyes and grow rapidly, making them large, meat-type geese. When mature, the gander can weigh close to 30 pounds. They make excellent barnyard alarms, as they can be protective of their territory and flock. They can be aggressive, especially ganders protecting his flock, so small children and pets should be watched when around a flock. Male Emden goslings have a lighter gray down than the female goslings. The goose can lay up to 40 eggs during the breeding season. It is also a good breed for a crossbreeding program, as these geese mature early and are good foragers for food — and the females are good mothers.

Toulouse: The Toulouse is a large breed and may weigh up to 25 pounds. It is noted for its cold tolerance and is a popular breed in the Midwest, although it has its origins in France. The Toulouse breed has dark gray feathers on its back, lighter gray feathers on its breast, and white stomach feathers. It has a dewlap or flap of skin hanging under its lower jaw and a bulky body. The Toulouse was bred in France to produce foie gras. As such, it is not as good a forager as other geese breeds and does well when confined to a pen. The goslings also mature slower than other breeds. The goose lays about 35 eggs per year and is a good mother. However, they can be clumsy and break eggs if the nest is not well-padded.

Chinese goose

Chinese: This breed is the smallest of domestic geese. They have been called Swan Geese, as they carry their body up-right (similar to swans). They are distinctive geese because they have a knob at the base of their beak. The knob on the male is larger than on the female. Chinese geese come in two colors: brown and white. The white variety has a more attractive carcass, as their pinfeathers are not as noticeable. Another added trait is they make excellent weeders, eating weeds from vegetable crops without causing much damage to the vegetables due to their smaller size and better agility at moving. Female Chinese geese will lay 50–60 eggs during the breeding season (February through June). The Chinese goose makes a good guard goose for the farmstead.

African: The African goose is related to the Chinese goose, but it is a much larger breed. It has a distinctive knob on its forehead near the bill and a dewlap. It is about the same size and weight as the Emden breed. The colored variety of African has brown top feathers and a lighter underbelly. The White African variety has white feathers and orange bill, knob, legs, and feet. Despite its name, it does not come from Africa, but its origin is murky. A mature gander weighs 22–24 pounds, while a mature female weighs 18–20 pounds. They can start breeding their first year and can produce eggs for many years. They lay around 35–40 eggs a year.

Pilgrim: The Pilgrim goose breed was developed in Iowa but may have had origins in colonial America. They can be easily sexed from their feather coloring; adult males have mostly white feathers, while females have gray feathers. This trait is called auto-sexing. Even when a day old, the breed can be sexed on color: male goslings are gray-yellow with light bills, and female goslings are olive-gray with dark bills. This is a medium-sized breed, with mature males weighing 14–5 pounds. It is also a calmer breed than most of the goose breeds but will still sound an alarm at perceived signs of danger. They are good foragers and good mothers. The female lays 35–40 eggs each year.

Sebastopol: This unique breed has blue eyes and curly, twisted feathers that are usually white. Due to their unique feathers, they should have bathing water available to keep their feathers clean. Because of their feather pattern, they are more susceptible to chilling. Unlike other geese, water does not roll off the feathers. They are a gentle breed of goose and are not aggressive. This makes them more susceptible to predation. Females can lay around 40 eggs a year and will brood the eggs of other geese. In fact, they may steal eggs from other nests and roll them into their own. Female goslings have darker down than the males. Ganders weigh around 14 pounds, and females average about 11 pounds.

Starting Out on the Right Foot

Ducklings or goslings are purchased the same places as chickens: directly from the hatchery or through feed stores. They will come in a straight run (both sexes), or they can be sexed if you want to have more of one sex. Generally, a straight run will be a few cents cheaper to purchase than those segregated by sex. For the average small-scale farmer, a straight run will be satisfactory for ducks or geese raised for meat. Males generally will be heavier than females. If you want to breed ducks and geese, you may want them sexed so you can have a proper ratio of males to female. One drake will breed five to six females. Most ganders will only breed with one or two females.

When purchasing your ducklings and gosling directly from the hatchery, ask when they will be mailed. It is safe to ship newly hatched waterfowl, as long as they are properly packaged in sturdy cardboard containers with plenty of air holes. They can go without food for a day or two while being shipped, as after hatching they retain part of the yolk from the egg in their body. This will give them a food source.

Make sure someone is home to receive the ducklings or goslings when they arrive in the mail. Open the shipping container in the presence of the mail carrier to ensure you have received the number of birds ordered and to check for any dead stock. If the number is less than expected or if there are any dead birds, the postal carrier can give you a claim check to submit to the hatchery. If you chose to purchase your stock from a store, closely scrutinize the conditions of their pen. It should be dry, and the feed and water containers should be clean and full. The ducklings and goslings should be active, if awake, with no noticeable discharge from their eyes or nose. Take a peek under their tails. The vent (anus) should be clean with no build-up of fecal material.

Ducklings and goslings should be raised separately because of the goslings' larger size. However, general care is similar, so the material presented in this chapter will apply to both species.

Preparing for your new arrivals

Prior to ordering or heading to the feed store to purchase your new additions, the pen, feeders, and waterers should be set up and ready. The pen should be in a draft-free, fully enclosed building with good ventilation and lighting. A corner of a garage or barn will work as well, provided you keep running motors out of the area so the birds are not subjected to fumes. You should allow 6 inches of space per bird. Increase this to 1 foot per bird after they are 2 weeks old to add more space for the birds as they grow.

The pen floor should be covered with an absorbent litter. Four inches of wood shavings, peat moss, or chopped straw will be sufficient. The litter will need to be maintained to eliminate wet, dirty spots. Add fresh litter as needed to maintain 4 inches of bedding. Heat and light can be provided through use of a heat lamp with a 250-watt bulb, or a hover brooder can be used. A hover brooder uses propane heat coupled with a metal pan (or hover) to direct and retain the heat over the young. Plan on using one heat lamp per 15 goslings or 25 ducklings. Hover brooders typically come with instructions for chicks. But because ducklings and goslings are larger than chicks, brood one-half as many ducklings and one-third as many goslings as you would chicks.

The heat-source temperature should be between 85 and 90°F. This temperature can be reduced 5 to 10 degrees every week until the temperature is around 70°F. After the sixth week — and if the weather is mild — the birds will be fully feathered and will no longer need supplemental heat. The birds should be confined near the heat, feed, and water sources during the first two to three days after arrival. Observe the birds closely to determine if the heat source needs to be raised or lowers. As with chickens, if the birds avoid the heat source and are lurking at the edges of the pen, raise the heat source a few inches. If they huddle under the heat source, lower it a few inches.

Waterers should be full when the birds arrive. There are many types of reasonably priced waterers available. Do not use an open pan for young ducklings or goslings; they should not get wet when they are in the down stage, lest they become chilled. A chilled baby bird can quickly become hypothermic and die. Instead, use a waterer with a base wide enough in which the birds can dip their heads and bills. Adding commercial electrolyte or vitamin powder to the water the first few days can give the young birds a healthy boost.

Do not let young ducks or geese have access to swimming water, and do not leave them outside in the rain. The feathers of young ducks and geese are not fully developed to protect them from water, especially during the down stage. If they have been hatched out by a mother duck or goose, they can have access to swimming water with the adults because the mother will not let them remain in the water for too long, and she will protect them from rain. By 4 or 5 weeks, the ducklings will be feathered out and will be able to tolerate most weather conditions. Goslings can be placed on pasture around 6 weeks of age in good weather.

Feeding

A good commercial starter feed will get your young goslings and ducklings off to a good start. They are generally disease-resistant, so a medicated feed will not be necessary. In fact, certain medications found in chick starters can cause health problems in goslings and ducklings. After four weeks, their diet can be supplemented with cracked corn, and they can be switched to a grower ration. Starting the first week of life, small amounts of fresh growing grass or fresh clippings can also be fed to the birds.

A plot of pasture enclosed by a 3-foot, woven-wire fence makes a great feed source for the birds when they are about 6 weeks old. Both ducks and geese are great at foraging bugs and plants. An acre of pasture can support up to 40 ducks or 20 geese. Geese are larger than ducks and will need more pasture, or they will quickly become defoliated and heavily soiled. By the time goslings are 6 weeks old, most of their diet can consist of forage, provided the pasture is in a succulent stage. They do not care for alfalfa or tough, narrow-leaved grasses. Good plants for pasture are brome grass, timothy, orchard grass, bluegrass, and clover. Water should be readily available, along with a source for the geese and ducks to bathe. If you have fewer than 10 birds, you can use a hose or a small children's pool to provide drinking and bathing water. This will need twice-daily cleaning and refilling. If you have more birds, provide separate waterers and bathing tubs. A small pond can be used for bathing, but the banks can quickly become damaged if too many ducks or geese are stocked on the pond.

If your geese or ducks are to be slaughtered for home use or for market, they should be fed a finishing ration formulated for turkeys, starting one month prior to slaughter. This will provide them extra nutrients, allowing them to fatten prior to slaughter.

Birds not intended for slaughter do not need to be fed a finishing ration.

Health Concerns

Although waterfowl are fairly disease-resistant, infectious diseases can and do take a toll on unlucky flocks. To keep your ducks and geese as disease-free as possible, try to limit their contact with wild birds that can carry viruses and bacteria from an infected flock to yours. Another strategy to minimize disease is to keep your birds' water source, feed, and pens clean of droppings. If feeders or waterers become soiled with feces, a good scrubbing with bleach water (1 teaspoon bleach per gallon water) will help kill disease organisms. Allow the cleaned equipment to dry before refilling with feed or water.

If you plan on pasturing your flock, make sure there is enough ground for the birds. Overstocking pens and pastures is an invitation for disease organisms in the feces to grow and multiply. Rotating pastures through use of small paddocks will be beneficial in two ways: Fecal material will get a chance to dry, and the action of sunlight can neutralize many disease organisms. It will also give the pasture plants a chance to grow back.

Here are some common diseases that can affect ducks and geese:

Avian influenza: This is the disease that has caused much concern throughout the world. Avian influenza affects both ducks and geese. The mild form causes such signs as lethargy, trouble breathing, diarrhea, and loss of appetite. Death losses are rare from the mild form of avian influenza, but the more severe form can cause death of the entire flock and is characterized by the above signs plus facial swelling. There is no specific treatment for avian influenza aside from good husbandry, and there is not a vaccination. Prevention includes strict attention to rodent control, disinfection of boots and equipment, and control of wild birds. Humans have also been affected by avian influenza.

Botulism: Ducks can be affected by botulism, otherwise known as limber neck. The disease is caused by the bacterium *Clostridium botulinum*, which grows in the mud and vegetation in warm, stagnant water. The duck ingests the bacteria, and it releases a toxin. The bird may be found dead, or it may be paralyzed but conscious. Treatment is possible during the first 24 hours by force-feeding the duck water and feed. The bird should be placed in a shaded, dry nest away from predators while the toxin wears off.

Chlamydiosis: Ducks are susceptible to chlamydiosis, or parrot fever. Signs of an infected duck include nose and eye discharges, sinus infections, reddened eyes, diarrhea, weight loss, and loss of appetite. The disease is spread from infected bird to healthy bird from discharges and feces. Wild birds can spread the disease to domestic ducks. Chlamydiosis is also spread through contaminated boots, clothing, and equipment. Once an infected duck recovers, it can still be a carrier of the organism. Treatment is through the use of the antibiotic chlortetracycline.

Fowl cholera: This infectious disease is caused by the bacterium *Pasteurella multocida*. Both ducks and geese can contract this disease, which strikes suddenly and causes numerous deaths in the flock. Factors that can cause an outbreak include overcrowded pens or ponds, spread of the disease from wild birds, and cold and damp weather. Though sudden death is usually the first sign of the disease, some birds will have convulsions, rapid breathing, become listless, have nasal discharge, or have vents matted with droppings. Treatment for those birds in the flock not ill from fowl cholera is the use of an antibiotic in the water. All sick birds should be removed from the flock and treated elsewhere. Dead carcasses should be burned.

Fowlpox: This disease can cause disease in ducks of all ages. There are two forms of fowlpox: The wet form causes canker-sore-like lesions in the mouth and throat, causing trouble breathing due to obstruction of these respiratory passages; the dry form causes raised, bumpy growths on the legs. It can cause problems with growth and egg production. Mosquitoes carry and spread this disease, thus spraying for mosquitoes can help control the spread. Vaccination is suggested if fowlpox becomes a problem in your flock.

Infectious hepatitis: This disease affects young ducklings between 2 and 3 weeks old. A virus that is either ingested or inhaled by waterfowl causes this disease. The sick duckling appears to be unable to gain its balance lying on its side with its head drawn back toward the tail. Their legs will also make paddling motions. Most cases result in death within a day of signs. Vaccinations are available for healthy ducklings in an infected flock, and mothers can also be vaccinated two weeks prior to laying eggs to pass immunity on to the ducklings.

Intestinal parasites: Different types of intestinal parasites can affect geese and ducks. Coccidiosis, roundworms, flukes, and tapeworms are ingested by the birds from the ground or feed contaminated with feces. Signs of infection are varied and range from young geese with stunted growth, lethargic birds, diarrhea, or death if the bird(s) are heavily infected. If you suspect your flock has intestinal parasites, a sample of feces should be taken to your veterinarian. The sample will be examined for parasites. Once the parasite is identified, treatment is through medication in the feed or water.

Salmonellosis: The bacterium *salmonella*, an organism that can affect a wide variety of animals and humans, causes this disease. It can quickly become a flock-wide problem due to its tendency to spread quickly. Signs of salmonellosis include lethargy, diarrhea, swollen joints, and lameness. Identification of the disease is only made through laboratory testing of feces from infected birds and examination of carcasses of dead or dying birds. A bird that survives salmonellosis will remain infected for life, and it should be separated from the rest of the flock to prevent spread of the disease.

Handling aggressive ganders

Ganders raised and imprinted on humans can become aggressive toward humans, since they view us as rivals for mates. This may happen at around 5 months of age. They will display dominant signs such as putting their heads down, pointing their bill up, or spreading their wings out. Sometimes humans who tease or chase geese can provoke this behavior as well. Do not allow children or immature adults to harass your geese.

If a gander does display such behavior toward you, you will need to confront it immediately before it becomes a major problem. Step toward the bird. He should back off, but if he does not, loosely grab a wing. You will need to work quickly, as the gander may try to bite you when you attempt this maneuver. When he tries to back off, let go of the wing. He may try to intimidate you a few times, but it is important for you to confront the gander each time he tries to be the dominant figure. If this behavior continues unchecked, it will turn into a major problem every time you come around the flock.

If you do have an aggressive gander, you can try to get the upper hand by grabbing him and pinning him to the ground. His wings will flap (and they can pack a punch), and he may bite you. He definitely will squawk, but keep him down until he submits by resting. Then let him go and repeat as necessary until he leaves you alone. Wearing heavy leather gloves, safety glasses, and a jacket will help protect you from his wings and bill.

Breeding

Ducks and geese intended for breeding should have a wing or leg band applied so you can identify them when you breed them. Banding should be done soon after hatching, and each band used on one animal should have identical numbers. Records should be kept regarding the parents of each duck, how many eggs each duck or goose lays, if she is broody and for how long, and how many eggs are hatched for each female. Poorly performing ducks and geese can be identified by their band and culled.

The tail features of ducks descended from Mallards will help you determine the sex. Drakes will have a few curled feather tips at the end of their tails, while females' tails will lie flat. Geese are not so easily identified as adults. They should be purchased as sexed and banded as soon as possible so you can tell gander from goose. For those breeds that cannot be sexed on physical characteristics (for example, Pilgrims by feather color, Emden by down color, and Chinese by beak knob), vent sexing will need to be done. This is performed when the ducklings or goslings are a couple of days old.

The bird is held with the vent facing the person performing the sexing. The right thumb and first finger are placed on either side of the vent and pressed firmly over it. The vent is then parted slowly to expose the inner lining. The left thumb is used to gently pull back on the skin surrounding the vent. This will expose a pink-colored cloaca, and the penis (a small protuberance) in the male will be visible. The females have a genital eminence — a small fold of tissue. Adults are sexed in a similar manner but will struggle when caught.

Only those ducks and geese in good physical shape should be kept for breeding. Legs should be straight and free of deformities, as should the beak and wings. They should comply with breed standards for coloring, body shape, and weight. A drake can breed five to eight females. For geese, one gander should only be used for one or two females. Ducks can be bred during the first year; geese should be 1 year old when they breed. Geese prefer to mate on water, and the water should be deep enough for the geese to swim in.

Most duck eggs take 28 days to hatch, with the exception of Muscovy duck eggs, which take 35 days. If the female incubates her own eggs, make sure she has water and feed available near the nest. Pekin and Indian Runner ducks do not make good egg sitters, so you may need to have a foster mother incubate the eggs. Duck eggs can be brooded by broody chicken hens, but the eggs will need to be sprinkled with water every day. If you plan to artificially incubate the eggs, the process is similar to chickens except for differences in humidity and temperature. Incubation requires 99.5°F and 55–75 percent humidity. The eggs need to be turned at least twice daily, but preferably four times a day. At day 25, the temperature should be lowered and the humidity slightly increased. Once the ducklings are hatched, allow them to dry in the incubator for one hour. Then they can be moved to their prepared brooding pen.

Geese eggs take 30 days to hatch. Temperature in a forced-air incubator should be at 100°F; while in a still-air incubator, the temperature should be maintained at 103°F. The humidity should be at 50 to 55 percent for the first 27 days of incubation. Eggs should be turned 180 degrees four to six times each day. The final three days before hatching, the humidity should be increased to 75 percent. When the goslings hatch, the doors to the incubator should be opened to allow the humidity to escape; this allows the goslings' down to dry. After an hour, they should be dry and can be moved to the brooding pen.

Using Waterfowl for Weed Control, Insect Control, and as Alarms

Because of the goose's large size, excellent vision, and loud voice — and because of some breeds tend to be aggressive — they make good guard birds. Geese are fairly intelligent and have a good memory. They remember people or animals that scare, harass, or frighten them. They also remember troublesome and scary situations. These factors make the goose a good guard bird against intruders. Geese have a preferential appetite for grasses and will avoid eating broad-leaved plants, making them ideal weeders for gardens or vineyards. Before chemical weed control became commonplace, specialty crop growers relied on geese to keep the grass picked in such crops as asparagus, mint, beets, beans, onions, and potatoes. To use geese for weeding gardens, the garden rows should be at least one foot apart, and a fence should enclose the garden.

Let the geese have access to the garden once the plants have established themselves, and the geese will eradicate the grasses and small, tender weeds. For plants that ripen above ground, like tomatoes, do not allow the geese to weed these plants when the vegetables are ripe as they might peck at the colorful plants. Geese prefer to eat grasses (weeds) over vegetables, so remove them once the weeds have been eaten to keep them from sampling the vegetables. If snails and slugs are a garden problem, ducks can be let into the area to feast on these garden pests. Ducks are also good algae- and insect-eaters in ornamental ponds. However, do not stock the pond too heavily, or they may deposit too much feces in the water and destroy all plant life.

CASE STUDY: WHY WATERFOWL?

Suzanne Peterson
Azariah Acres Farm
Foley, Minnesota
www.azariahacres.net

Suzanne Peterson raises geese and ducks on her farm, Azariah Acres, near Foley, Minnesota. Peterson grew up on a hobby farm, where she learned that she really enjoyed caring for animals. Her love of animal husbandry led her to start farming for the joy of seeing animals grow.

Her first foray into farm birds was with chickens, but she found the market for small, farm-raised chickens very competitive. In 2008, she had the opportunity to raise geese and ducks. She found a market for these two species and that they are easier to raise than chickens. Peterson markets her birds as already-butchered birds at a local farmers' market.

Although Peterson feels ducks and geese are easier to keep than chickens, there are still many chores associated with waterfowl. She spends about an hour a day caring for her 15 geese and 80 ducks, including feeding, cleaning pens and waterers, thawing waterers in the winter, and clipping their wings to keep them contained. Recordkeeping is also an important chore. Peterson keeps records on when babies are hatched, how much feed the birds consume, each bird's weight at the butcher, and any disease or malformation issues.

Good fences are also a must, as predators — such as dogs and coyotes — can decimate a flock. Cats, possums, owls, and hawks can also snatch young ducks and geese. Finding a sick or injured bird is the worst part of raising geese. However, she rarely has disease problems with her birds, as she gives them ample access to water year-round and provides them plenty of pasture and pen space — the most important part of keeping disease out of a flock.

"The best aspect to raising ducks and geese is their intelligence and hardiness," Peterson said. "They are really interesting and beautiful animals." She feels raising geese and ducks could be a good family project if the birds are handled a lot. If not, she feels a child under 10 should not be around geese, because they are very strong and can be aggressive. However, if the animals are handled a lot, even a young child could help with the ducks and geese. Peterson suggests a beginner waterfowl farmer start with two to four geese or 20 ducks to get a good idea of the care needed for these birds.

CHAPTER 4

Keeping Turkeys and Game Birds

> ## *Terms To Know*
>
> **Poult:** A young turkey.
>
> **Snood:** A flap of skin hanging over the beak of a turkey.
>
> **Caruncle:** A brightly colored throat tissue on a turkey.
>
> **Wattle:** A flap of skin directly under the chin of a turkey.
>
> **Tom:** Male turkey.
>
> **Hen:** Female turkey.

The Modern Turkey

The modern turkey has undergone tremendous change due to the commercial turkey industry. Unlike their wild brethren, domesticated turkeys are much heavier and have a greater muscle mass. Through selective breeding, commercial strains of turkeys have massive muscles on a normal-sized frame. Their muscles have become so massive that most commercial strains can no longer breed naturally. The tom is unable to perform the act of mating with the hen, so eggs remain unfertile. Most commercial breed hens are mated through artificial insemination. The majority of commercial growers raise the variety of turkey called the Broad Breasted White. This is not an official breed; rather, it is a commercial variety of the Bronze turkey breed. There are other breeds that are not so highly bred, which you may find suitable for your small-scale farm. These will be discussed in the breed section of this chapter so you can find the turkey breed most suitable for your small-scale farm.

Turkeys are naturally inquisitive and friendly birds, although when mature, they can be a bit territorial and terrorize pets and small children if they are not trained to respect humans. Grabbing the turkey and pinning it to the ground can accomplish this, but be careful not to let them spur you in the process. Turkeys have some unique body parts. The caruncle is a brightly colored growth on the throat. The snood is the flap of skin that hangs over the beak. The wattle is a flap of skin right under the turkey's chin. The caruncle, snood, and wattle turn red when the turkey is feeling agitated or taking part in courtship.

One further note on turkeys: They should not be raised with chickens, as chickens can carry the organism responsible for the disease blackhead, which is further discussed in this chapter. Blackhead does not affect chickens, but it is a highly fatal disease in turkeys.

Guineas

The domesticated guinea fowl is descended from wild guinea fowl from Africa, specifically the country of Guinea. They have been domesticated for centuries and were used as a prize food source by the ancient Greeks and Romans. In addition to their meat, guineas are useful farm birds. They are territorial and emit loud, harsh calls if they sense danger or if someone new comes onto the property. Many people keep guineas to keep the insect and tick populations down, although these birds will also seek and destroy small reptiles and snakes. They will roam through gardens, leaving flowers and vegetables alone, in their quest to eat insects and weed seeds. During the night, they should be penned, as owl, hawks, and other predators will attack guineas.

Guineas are brooded and fed similar to turkeys up until they are around 6 weeks old. After that age, they can be allowed access to an outside run. Unlike turkeys, they can be kept with chickens and fed the same feed as chickens. If the pen is uncovered, the guineas will eventually fly out. Keeping food in the pen will entice them to return to roost at night so they can be shut inside. If you do not want your guineas to roam to protect them from predators, newly hatched keets can be pinioned (the last joint of the wing is clipped off) to permanently ground them. Older birds can have their flight feathers clipped (a painless process) to keep them grounded. Of course, you can also keep the top covered so they cannot escape by flying.

Guinea hens will try to lay their eggs in a secluded spot outside their pens. These nests can be difficult to find, but her mate will frequently hang around the hidden nest. Keep your hens in the pen if you want to collect the eggs or if you want her to hatch out the keets. Guinea eggs can be eaten just like chicken eggs. They are much larger, though, so recipes will need to be adjusted. One guinea egg equals approximately two chicken eggs.

If you plan to breed your guineas, one male can mate with five to six females. However, in the wild, they do prefer to mate with only one female because they are more secluded and selective. Guineas used for breeding should be penned. The pen should be covered or their wings should be clipped, to keep the hens from making nests in grassy areas. Guinea hens are not the best mothers and will lay their nests where predators can find the eggs or newly hatched keets. They will also lead their keets through wet grass. This will cause the keets to become wet and chilled, and they will die from exposure.

Turkey Breeds

The commercial varieties of the Broad Breasted White can be purchased from turkey hatcheries. These birds, if they have a constant source of feed, can grow to market weight of more than 30 pounds in 18 weeks. There are other breeds that are grouped under the term heritage breeds, which will take longer to grow to market weight, about 24 to 30 weeks. The heritage breeds are those turkeys that have been bred and raised for many decades. Many heritage breeds are in danger of extinction, as their total population numbers are low. Some people prefer these breeds for the table, claiming they have a better taste than the commercial varieties.

Beltsville Small White: This is a small, white turkey breed. Its white feathering means there are fewer visible pinfeathers than in the colored turkey breeds, and its smaller frame is popular with those consumers wanting a smaller framed table bird. Adult males average 23 pounds, and adult females average 13 pounds.

Black: This breed has greenish-black feathers. It is rare in North America, but it is bred in Europe, where it is considered to be a great table meat bird. Both Spain and England claim its development. Adult males commonly weigh 27 pounds, while an adult female weighs in at 18 pounds.

Blue Slate: This turkey has an ashy blue color, which is sometime splashed with black dots. Adult males weigh 30 pounds, and adult females weigh 18 pounds. This breed is listed as critical for extinction.

Bourbon Red: As its name suggests, this handsome bird has rich red feathers with wing and tail fans tipped with white. Adult males weigh 33 pounds and adult females weigh 18 pounds. It was developed in Kentucky and was an important commercial turkey in the 1930s and 1940s.

Bronze: The broad-breasted Bronze variety has massive breast muscles and can be either bronze or white. There is an unimproved variety, but it is rarely bred. Adult males weigh 36 pounds, and adult females weigh 20 pounds.

Narragansett: This turkey has gray, tan, black, and white feathers in a similar pattern to the Bronze turkey. It was developed in the Eastern United States and named for the Narragansett Bay in Rhode Island. Adult males weigh between 22 and 28 pounds, while hens weigh 12–16 pounds.

Royal Palm: Unlike most turkey breeds, the Royal Palm turkey was bred more for its unique look than for its meat production. It primarily has white feathers, with black feathers stippling the breast and covering a wide swath along the base of the tail. The tail feathers have a wide band of black a few inches from the tail tips. An adult male averages 22 pounds, and an adult female averages 12 pounds.

White Holland: As the name suggests, this is a white-feathered turkey. It is a large bird, with adult males weighing 25 pounds and adult females weighing 16 pounds. It was an important commercial bird in the early 1900s, but its numbers have declined to the point that it is threatened with extinction today.

Guinea Breeds

Guineas are very handsome fowl. They have a helmet, which is a bony ridge on the head, and they have small wattles. They weigh about 3 ½ pounds when full-grown. Their eggs are small and dark. Adult males are distinguished from adult females by the larger helmet and wattles of the males and the male's coarser head. A male guinea will also screech louder than females. There are three varieties of guineas based on feather color:

Pearl: This variety has purple-gray feathers with small, white dots (pearls).

White: As its name suggests, the White guinea has pure white plumage.

Lavender: The Lavender guinea has lighter gray/purple feathers than the Pearl variety. It also is splashed with small, white dots.

Housing

Poults and keets will need to be confined and carefully monitored to decrease losses during their early life. Like other domesticated poultry, the young can suffer from cold weather, disease, and lack of water or food intake. The first few weeks — until they are fully feathered out — are the most critical in the life of poults and keets.

Confinement

You will need to allow 20 square feet per mature bird when you plan for turkey housing needs. Guineas will need half this amount if you plan to keep them confined. Part of this housing could consist of an outside run — a fenced-in area that allows the birds to have access to fresh air and sunlight. Even if you provide an outdoor run for your birds, the building will need to be ventilated. This can be as simple as having a few windows that can be propped open to an exhaust fan installed in the wall. Ammonia fumes from manure can build up if the bedding is not cleaned frequently. This can lead to losses due to respiratory distress and infection.

Young turkeys and keets need to stay dry and warm. This can be accomplished by using a layer of wood shavings, chopped straw, or sawdust on the floor for bedding. Turkeys are very curious and might peck at the bedding instead of their feed the first few days. Some producers will cover the bedding with cloth or paper to keep the poults from eating the litter. This can be removed in a few days when you are certain all the young turkeys are eating the feed provided and are more interested in eating the feed than tasting the bedding.

A corral, made from 18-inch cardboard or straw bales, can be used to confine the poults or keets in the feeding and drinking area for the first few days. It is also a useful strategy to keep the birds near the heat source. A heat lamp with a 250-watt light bulb will be sufficient. It should be hung so the bottom of the bulb is about a foot above the young birds' heads, adjusting as needed if the birds huddle under the light by lowering the heat lamp or if they stay away from the bulb by raising heat lamp.

Place plenty of feeders and waterers down for the new poults and keets — two each for every ten poults or 25 keets should be sufficient. Observe the birds closely the first day or two to make sure they find the food and water. Feed a commercial starter mix to the birds to ensure they get all the nutrients they need. You can purchase turkey starter mix from a feed store or grain elevator. After the birds are eating well, the feeders should be placed on bricks or hung up to keep the birds from spilling the feed onto the floor. Raise the feeders enough so that the bird's heads are higher than their rears when feeding. One-gallon waterers are good for starting the young poults, but you will soon find you will need larger waterers to satisfy these fast-growing, large birds' thirst.

Turkeys on range

Turkeys, particularly the heritage breeds, do well when fed on pasture. To start, plan on stocking 100 birds for each acre of land. The best forages to plant for a turkey pasture are legumes, like alfalfa or clovers, and grasses like Timothy grass, orchard grass, or rye grass. The area you plan to raise your turkeys in should be fenced in with woven wire, with openings small enough so the young turkeys cannot escape. A shelter large enough to house all the turkeys at once so they do not crowd should also be provided in case of poor weather.

Feeders should be provided and scattered throughout the field so turkeys do not crowd around them and destroy the surrounding pasture. They should also be covered to prevent rain from damaging the feed and raised from the ground so they are level with the turkey's backs. You should plan to allow 6 inches of feeder space per bird. Trough-type feeders are good for the range because turkeys can access each side. Even if you only have a few birds, you should have at least two feeders available to prevent one turkey from bullying weaker ones away from the feed. Feed will need to be provided in order for your turkeys to properly grow. Do not feed turkeys chicken feed because they have different vitamin and mineral requirements than chickens. If you cannot find turkey feed in your area, you can substitute game bird food. Food should be available to the turkeys on a free choice basis to allow your turkeys to grow as quickly as their genetic makeup permits.

Waterers should also be scattered throughout the pasture area. These should be cleaned frequently with a bleach solution or a disinfectant. Fresh water needs to be available at all times. Five adult turkeys will drink 1 gallon of water daily, so plan the number of waterers accordingly. During warmer weather the turkeys will drink more, so check the water supply twice daily to make sure they do not run out.

Partridge, Pheasants, and Quail

These three species of bird can be a valuable niche product, provided a marketing plan is carefully thought-out prior to stepping into the game bird market. Most of these birds will be sold directly to local consumers or hunting preserves. Quails, partridge, and pheasants are raised for release during the hunting season, although you should contact your local Department of Fish and Wildlife prior to release of birds into the wild. They are also raised for showing at exhibitions.

The Chukar partridge is native to Eurasia. This beautiful bird has orange-red legs, feet, and bill, with grayish feathers. It also has a black band across the forehead, around the eyes, and down the neck. They are fairly calm birds and are easy to raise for hunting release or meat.

The Chinese Ring-necked pheasant is a beautiful bird imported into North America as a game bird. It quickly established a large population in the wild. Roosters are very showy, with metallic red, brown, and green body feathers and metallic blue, green and black head feathers. A white ring of feathers encircles the neck. Hens are a dull brown color. The Mongolian pheasant is larger than the Chinese pheasant and has an incomplete neck ring. The

Mongolian pheasant has more meat than the Chinese and is often raised as a table-meat bird.

Bobwhite quail are native to the eastern part of North America, while the Japanese quail has been domesticated in Japan for thousands of years. It reaches sexual maturity very early, at 6 weeks of age, and lays heavy eggs, considering its size. Bobwhites are very well-adapted to being raised for meat and egg production.

Incubating eggs

Species	Days of Incubation
Chukar partridge	23–24
Hungarian partridge	24–25
Bobwhite quail	23–24
Japanese quail	17–18
Chinese Ring-necked pheasant	23–24
Mongolian Ring-necked pheasant	24–25

Game bird eggs can be purchased from breeders and incubated much like chicken eggs. Incubated eggs should be clean, free from cracks, and not abnormally shaped. The incubator should be cleaned and disinfected. It should be set at the desired temperature and humidity, and should run 24 hours prior to placing the eggs inside. Always read the instructions that come with your particular brand of incubator, especially on how to ventilate the incubator, as well as to read temperature and humidity levels. The eggs should be turned at least three times daily. Marking the eggs with a permanent marker will help you remember which sides of the eggs were last turned. When the chicks start to hatch, the incubator temperature should be decreased. Remove chicks from the incubator when 95 percent of the hatched chicks are dry.

Incubator Type	Incubation Temperature*	Humidity	Hatch Temperature*
Still air	102°–103°F	60%	100°–101°F
Fan	99.5°–100°F	60%	98.5°F

Temperature will vary based on location. Figures are an estimate.

Housing

After the young are removed from the incubator they should go into the prepared brooding pen. Much like other brooding pens it should be set up prior to placing them into the pen. You will need a heat and light source; a heat lamp will provide both of these necessities. If your brooding pen is a rectangular or square shape, the corners should be rounded with cardboard or wire to prevent the chicks from crowding and smothering each other. All equipment used in the brooder should be disinfected, either with bleach water (1 teaspoon per gallon) or with a commercial disinfecting solution. Allow the equipment to dry thoroughly before use. Three to four inches of clean bedding should be placed on the pen floor. Wood shavings, rice or peanut hulls, ground corncobs, or chopped straw make acceptable bedding. The tops of an open pen should be covered with chicken wire or mesh to keep predators out and, when the birds feather out, to keep them inside.

The heat source should be lowered so it is 2 inches over the young. This will need to be carefully monitored the first day. If they are scattered away from the heat source, raise it an inch or two. If they are huddled beneath the heat source, it should be slightly lowered. Ideally, the temperature under the heat source should be 95°F. This temperature should be maintained for the first week, then the heat can be lowered 5°F each week until it is 70°F. The first few days you may want to confine the chicks close to the heat source with a small cardboard or wire ring to prevent them from wandering into the cooler parts of the brooding pen. A light should be on continuously during the first week; starting the second week, the light can be left on for 12 hours a day until the chicks are ready to be removed from the brooder. If the pen starts to smell of urine, or if there are any wet or excessively dirty spots, the bedding should be removed and refreshed with clean litter.

When the birds are fully feathered (around 6 weeks of age), they can be moved to growing cages or a flight pen. Partridge and quail can be kept in inside pens if being raised for food, but if they are raised for hunting they should be placed in a flight pen so they develop good flight muscles. Inside cages for these two species should allow for ½-square-foot of floor space for quail and 1-square-foot floor space for partridge. Pheasants should be raised in flight pens.

The flight pen is constructed in a long rectangular shape. It should be located in a quiet area of the farm, away from human and vehicle traffic. Plan accordingly to allow 3- to 4-square-feet per partridge or quail or 10-square-feet per pheasant. The pen should be built against a building to allow the birds to have access to the inside in case of poor weather. The sides are made of upright wood or steel posts and chicken wire. The wire should be sunk 18 inches into the ground along the base of the pen to prevent predators from tunneling into the pen. The top is covered with poultry netting to keep the birds from flying out. A low wall (24 inches) of boards around the pen's perimeter will provide further protection from wind.

Feeding

To start, a 1-gallon waterer should be placed for every 50 birds. Dip each bird's beak into the waterers when you place them into the brooding pen so they know where to find the water. Watch quail carefully around the waterers, as they are very tiny and can fall into the waterer bases. Placing some clean, small rocks into waterer's base the first few days will provide them with footing if they do fall into the water.

Game bird starter feed can be purchased from local farm stores or grain elevators and should be fed to chicks until they are 6 weeks old. They can also be fed a turkey starter ration, but regardless of starter, it should have 24–28 percent protein. After 4 weeks, you can add some whole grains to the diet as long as you also provide the birds with grit. From 6 weeks to 14 weeks, a game bird grower or turkey grower ration with 20 percent protein should be fed to the birds. After this, they can be fed a ration with 15 percent protein. Twenty inches of feeding space should be allowed per 100 chicks. Scatter some feed on pieces of cardboard or newspaper near the feeders the first few days so the chicks can find the feeder.

In the flight pen, vegetation should be planted to provide cover for the birds. By providing vegetation, twice as many birds can be grown than in pens without vegetation. This is because vegetation provides environmental enrichment and protection for birds that are being picked on by other birds. This can range from a few conifer trees to annual grasses like millet, oats, wheat, barley, or even weeds like pigweed or lambs quarter. Waterers and feeders should be scattered throughout the pen. Feeders should be covered to prevent moisture from damaging the feed.

Turkey Health

There are three diseases that are the primary culprits for turkeys getting sick. A helpful memory trick is to think of the letters ABC.

Airsacculitis: This is a disease that affects the turkey's air sacs. The respiratory system of a bird is very different from mammals. The lungs are attached to the inside of the rib cage, so there is no diaphragm to inflate and expand the lungs; instead, birds have a system of thin-walled pouches, or air sacs, that connect to the lungs by openings called ostia. The muscles that attach to the keel bone (breast bone) move this bone much like bellows during breathing. This changes the pressure in the air sacs to cause the lungs to draw in and expel air. Sometimes during the process of breathing, foreign material or microorganisms can become lodged in the air sacs. These substances cause inflammation and infection of the air sacs, which can lead to poor growth rate in a flock or even death. To prevent airsacculitis, ventilation in turkey houses should be carefully monitored. Buildup of ammonia fumes and opening windows or using exhaust fans will help to minimize dust particles that enter the turkey houses. Treatment for infected air sacs is through the use of antibiotics in the drinking water.

Blackhead: Blackhead, or histomoniasis, is a disease that primarily affects young turkeys. Microscopic protozoa, *Histomonas meleagridis*, cause damage to the liver and intestine of infected turkeys. If untreated, turkeys with blackhead will die. The disease is spread from a bird that has cecal worms infected with the protozoa. These infected cecal worms are passed through the feces to the ground. The protozoa reside in the cecal worm eggs that are then consumed by earthworms. The turkey usually becomes infected with histomoniasis through ingesting these earthworms that are infected with the eggs. Turkeys sick with histomoniasis will have dropped tails and ruffled feathers, and will act dull and depressed. If histomoniasis is suspected, the treatment is with the medication dimetridazole. If any turkeys are dead, they should be burned or buried to prevent contamination of the soil with cecal worm eggs. Equipment should be cleaned and disinfected as well. The soil in pens from an infected flock can remain contaminated for up to three years. A new site for a pen should be chosen if turkeys are raised on the same farm.

Coccidiosis: This disease is caused by parasites that cause decreased growth and death in turkeys. After ingesting the organism in feed or water contaminated with feces, it grows in the intestine and causes damage to tissues. This damage leads to decreased absorption of nutrients, decreased feed intake, blood loss, and an increased susceptibility to other infections. The primary symptoms are an outbreak of bloody diarrhea along with lethargic birds that huddle together with ruffled feathers. These outbreaks are usually related to an increased number of turkeys in a small space: the higher the stocking density, the greater the number of coccidia in a smaller area. This increases the chance that turkeys, through picking at the ground, will eat larger amounts of coccidia. Low levels of coccidia in the digestive tract will not cause much damage, but higher numbers will cause serious problems. It is usually a more severe problem in young birds. Treatment includes addition of coccidiostats — medications that kill coccidia — in the feed or water. Prevention relies on removing manure, moving birds to fresh ground, and decreasing stocking density in pens.

Other turkey diseases

Blue comb: Turkeys ingesting contaminated feed or water will be at risk for this disease. It affects the digestive tract, leading to loss of appetite, diarrhea, decreased body temperature, dehydration, and death. Poults are most severely affected and there is no treatment. Prevention revolves around strict sanitation of pens and equipment and keeping the young turkeys dry and warm.

Erysipelas: Erysipelas is caused by the bacterium *Erysipelothrix insidiosa*. The bacteria gain entry into the turkey's body through wounds and are found in the soil of many turkey farms. Turkeys affected with erysipelas will be lethargic, and will have a bluish discoloration to the head, sulfur-colored droppings, swelling of the snood, and nasal discharge. Erysipelas can be treated with antibiotics, and there is a vaccination available. The disease can also be passed on to humans, swine, and sheep. Use rubber gloves when treating sick birds.

Gapeworms: These parasites are primarily a problem of young birds raised on range. They gain entry into the bird's body when the birds eat earthworms, which harbor the gapeworm eggs. The worms become infected when they eat the eggs passed in the dropping of infected turkeys. In the turkey, the eggs develop into worms that reside in the lungs. The growing worms block the trachea and can cause them to suffocate. Signs include outstretched necks and coughing. The birds will not eat and quickly become weak. Birds can be treated with anthelmintics (dewormer) in the food or water. To prevent this from occurring, keep the food and water off the ground. If you have a problem, the soil in the pens can be tilled after the growing season to help destroy eggs.

Fowl lice and mites: There are numerous species of lice and mites that can affect all poultry. Though lice do not directly kill poultry, they can lead to discomfort and loss of productivity. They are usually straw-colored and can be found on the skin or on feathers. White lice egg clusters can be found attached at the base of the feathers. Mites can be of variable appearance but are generally very small, crawling insects on the bird. Treatment for both is through use of an insecticide formulated for poultry. The premises should also be treated to kill those insects hiding in cracks and crevices.

Pullorum disease: *Salmonella pullorum* is the bacterium that causes pullorum disease. It is spread from infected hens to their young through the shells and also from bird to bird through infected droppings. There is a high death rate among poults affected with pullorum disease; older birds can harbor a chronic infection. Signs of pullorum disease include lethargy, huddling, ruffled feathers, diarrhea that pastes the vent, no appetite, and weakness. It is not very common anymore due to nationwide efforts to eradicate the disease. If a turkey has pullorum, it should be reported to federal authorities, as the government is trying to eradicate the disease. Treatment is unsatisfactory, and infected premises are very difficult to free of the microorganism. Poults should be purchased from pullorum-free flocks and hatcheries.

Guinea Fowl Health

Guinea fowl are susceptible to many of the same diseases as chickens and turkeys, especially when they are still keets. One main cause of death of adult guinea that are allowed to free range is predation from owls, hawks, and coyotes, and from being run over by vehicles on roadways. Guinea hens allowed to nest outside of a designated pen will typically lose their keets due to predators and poor weather. To keep your guineas from roosting outside at night, you can clip their wings to keep them from flying out of their pens and to keep them out of trees. Clipping involves taking sharp scissors and cutting off half the length of the primary flight feathers. These are the last ten feathers on the wing. You should only cut the primary flight wings on one wing. When the bird molts, these feathers will grow back, so you will need to repeat the process after each molting session. This may mean reclipping the wing every few months for younger birds or a year for older birds.

Game Bird Health

While not a disease, one big cause of death among game birds raised in captivity is cannibalism. Pheasants are more prone to cannibalism, but all species and ages are capable of this vicious act. It may start as simple feather picking and can quickly explode into a full-blown attack to the death. There are many causes of cannibalism. These include:

- Overcrowding

- Territorial aggression

- External parasites

- Nutritional imbalances

- Injuries due to poorly maintained pens or equipment

- Poor sanitation and ventilation

- Too high of a brooding temperature

To help minimize the chance of cannibalism from occurring in your game bird flock, there are a few management steps you can take — however, even the best-managed flocks may still have problems. Provide the birds with adequate floor space, shelter, and eating and drinking space. Vegetation in flight pens will allow birds to escape and hide from the other aggressive birds. Maintaining the pen and equipment will cut down on chance of injuries, as well. Remove injured, sick, or weak birds from the flock as soon as they are observed. Work quietly among your birds to avoid frightening or startling them.

Game birds can be affected by many of the other diseases affecting poultry, such as coccidiosis, fowl pox, fowl cholera, erysipelas, blackhead, and internal and external parasites. Pheasants can be affected by marble spleen disease, a viral disease common in confinement-raised pheasants. With marble spleen disease, most birds are found dead. Necropsy (examination of the dead bird) shows an enlarged spleen with a mottled color along with fluid buildup in the lungs and other internal organs. There is a vaccination available to prevent flock losses. Quails are susceptible to a viral respiratory disease called quail bronchitis. Young quail are most severely affected with coughing, sneezing, and wheezing being the predominate signs. There is no vaccination available for this disease, which can cause the entire flock to be lost. To help prevent this disease, keep stray wild birds and rodents away from the flock through pen and building maintenance.

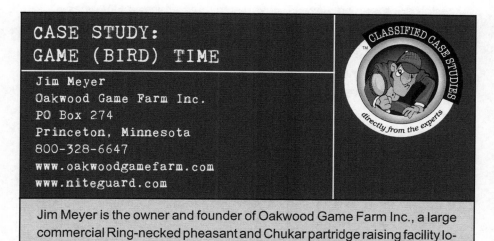

CASE STUDY: GAME (BIRD) TIME

Jim Meyer
Oakwood Game Farm Inc.
PO Box 274
Princeton, Minnesota
800-328-6647
www.oakwoodgamefarm.com
www.niteguard.com

Jim Meyer is the owner and founder of Oakwood Game Farm Inc., a large commercial Ring-necked pheasant and Chukar partridge raising facility located in east-central Minnesota. Founded in 1967, they currently hatch and ship thousands of day-old chicks and adults to customers across the country.

Meyer started his game farm with 50 day-old pheasant chicks. His business has grown to the point that Oakwood now raises 125,000 pheasants and 20,000 partridges on two farms. Oakwood Game Farm employs 20 people, and a few people are working around the clock, seven days a week, to care for the birds. They also market 400,000 chicks annually. Pheasants are raised for both release and eating, and are also sold at their retail store.

Meyer advises anyone interested in entering the game bird market to do their research prior to investing in game birds: A solid market for the birds should be identified. Raising game birds is very labor-intensive at all points in the process. Some major pitfalls to raising pheasants in particular are underestimating the amount of space needed to raise a quality bird, not having the correct cover on the flight pens, controlling predators, and preventing cannibalism.

Meyer keeps extensive records on all aspects of his business. This includes the number of eggs produced each day, number of eggs set, and number of chicks hatched. Other records include the number of chicks kept on the farms, death rates, feed consumption, medication usage, vaccinations, and blood test results. Records are also kept regarding customer orders, employees, advertising, budgeting, and finances.

"Raising pheasants is not for the weak of heart," Meyer said. "The birds retain much of their wildness, and this is a plus; however, it also can be a negative. Unlike chickens, when pheasants get loose — and they will — they fly away. That is like watching all of the hard work, cost, and potential profit fly into the sunset. Predators can — and they will — get into outside pens and kill many, many birds in a single night, and will return again and again. Ice and heavy wet snows will stick to your pen tops and collapse the entire structure, and give freedom to your birds or kill them. Having said all of that, the joy of raising a chick into a full-grown, beautiful rooster pheasant successfully, and then being able to sell it (and make some money) is quite a feat and gives a feeling of pride and satisfaction."

CHAPTER 5

Rearing Rabbits

Terms To Know

Buck: An adult male rabbit.

Coprophagia: The act of an animal in which it eats its own fecal matter. Rabbits need to do this to acquire needed nutrients.

Doe: An adult female rabbit.

Fryer: A young rabbit around 8 weeks old and 4 ½ pounds that is ready to be butchered.

Kindle (kindling): Term used to for rabbits giving birth.

Kit: A newborn or very young rabbit.

Raising rabbits can be a fun way to introduce mammals to a small-scale farm. As most people know, rabbits can multiply quickly, but like any animal, improper management can lead to loss due to sick animals and predation, and poor reproductive performance. Starting out with a small herd can expose you to the day-to-day management of rabbits to see if you really do have the stick-to-it attitude needed for rabbit production. The domestic rabbit we have today are all descendents of the wild European rabbit. It is believed that rabbits originated in what is now Spain. Rabbits were raised in ancient Rome for meat and pelts. The Romans are also thought to have selectively bred an Angora rabbit for its long hair to be used for yarn. During the Middle Ages, French monks practiced selective breeding in rabbits to maximize the desirable traits such as size and coat color. Rabbit pelts and meat were a valuable food and clothing source in the monasteries. From this start, different breeds were slowly developed until the 18th and 19th centuries, when breed development took off to the point that there are currently more than 100 breeds of rabbits worldwide.

Rabbits are cute and cuddly, and this trait might work against you when it comes time to selling or butchering the offspring of your breeding rabbits. Before you begin, you will want to do some market research to make sure you will be able to sell your stock at a profit — you would not want to invest the time and effort into raising rabbits if there are not people-ready to buy the meat or live rabbits. There may be a rabbit association in your state or region that can give you an idea of the demand for rabbit. Your county extension agent will be able to direct you to the right group. Once you link up with an association, ask them what breed of rabbit sells the best in your area. You should also ask if there is a nearby rabbit raiser who would let you tour their operation. They will also be a good source to inquire about new or used equipment dealers. Finding a market for your rabbits can be difficult, so start early and look hard for a reliable, steady sales outlook.

There are a few traits about rabbits that might surprise you. Most people are familiar with rabbit pellets — the rabbit's normal round stool. However, rabbits also pass a very soft stool, called a cecotrope, which is produced in the rabbit's cecum. The rabbit will eat the cecotrope — which is full of needed nutrients — and most rabbit owners may not even see this stool in the pen. This is a natural function and should not be confused with diarrhea.

Also, rabbits' hind legs are very powerful, giving this prey animal a powerful spurt of speed to outrun predators. Rabbits on open ground can reach speeds of 25 miles per hour when being pursued. Their front legs are also adapted for digging, either to dig a hole to hide from predators or to dig burrows to live in. In the wild, rabbits live in groups in a collection of burrows, or a warren. Rabbits are social animals, but they need to bond before they can live peacefully with other rabbits. They will fight over territory or mating, a trait that can make introducing new rabbits into an established group difficult.

A doe does not have regular heat periods or an estrus cycle. Instead, she will ovulate after mating. A doe can breed any time of the year, but she does have variable times where she will not accept a mating from a male rabbit. Purebred rabbits can be used as breeding stock to establish a small-scale young rabbit selling operation. Another business to explore is selling rabbit meat to specialty markets or gourmet restaurants. Rabbit-meat producers find that having 40 does will give them a good return on their investment. The rabbit manure can also be used as a fertilizer. Pelts can be sold or used for high-end fashions. A requirement for any small-scale farming business is to generate a reliable, healthy flow of rabbits. This can be accomplished by purchasing healthy stock, choosing the right breed of rabbits, keeping a breeding schedule, and maintaining your rabbits in the best health possible. To begin, you will need to decide which breed will fit best with your plans.

Breeds

There are more than 100 recognized breeds of rabbits. Rabbits range in size from the mini, which weigh as few as 2 pounds as adults, and up to the giant breeds, which can weigh more than 20 pounds. Here is a listing of some of the more common breeds of rabbits that you should be easily able to obtain to start up a small-scale rabbit raising operation:

Netherland Dwarf: The Netherland Dwarf is the smallest breed of rabbit, weighing in at only 2 pounds when full grown. It comes in a vast variety of colors. The Netherland Dwarf is primarily a pet rabbit due to its small size and its baby bunny-like appearance. Males can become dominant over much larger rabbits, but they can become very tame for people.

Dutch: The Dutch rabbit is an old breed developed in England. It comes in six colors: gray, tortoiseshell, steel, chocolate, brown, and black. All colors have a band of white around the chest, a wedge-shaped patch of white on the face, and white on the tips of the hind feet. The Dutch rabbit weighs around 4 pounds when mature. They make good pet rabbits.

American Sable: The American Sable is a beautiful, dark brown rabbit with darker coloring around the legs, ears, face, and tail. It weighs about 9 pounds when mature. The Sable makes a good meat and pelt production rabbit.

Angora: The Angora breed has actually four different sub-breeds of rabbits: the English Angora, Satin Angora, the French Angora, and the Giant Angora. The English Angora, despite its name, originated in Turkey. It comes in many colors and weighs about 6 pounds when mature. The Satin Angora has a silkier coat than the other types and weighs 7 pounds at maturity. The French Angora is similar to the English Angora in color but is heavier. The Giant Angora has the most fur of the Angoras. It weighs around 9 pounds when mature. All of these breeds have been valued for their fine fur production.

New Zealand: The New Zealand is a large rabbit, weighing about 10 pounds when mature. Its name is misleading, as it was developed in the United States. It is a very common rabbit used for meat and fur. It is also a popular animal used for scientific research purposes. This rabbit has red, black, or white fur.

Satin: This rabbit has a very soft and shiny fur coat. It comes in many different colors. The Satin weighs about 9 pounds when mature. In addition to their great pelt, they make good meat production rabbits.

Californian: The Californian rabbit is a large rabbit, weighing 9 pounds when mature. It has white fur, and its tail, feet, ears, and nose are black. It is a good meat-production rabbit.

Flemish Giant: This is the largest breed of rabbit. When mature, it will weigh more than 14 pounds; some rabbits are more than 22 pounds when full-grown. It is a popular pet rabbit and comes in a variety of colors.

Whichever breed you chose, you should carefully purchase your rabbits from a reputable breeder. You can find a listing of these breeders from state or regional rabbit associations, or by attending rabbit shows and asking exhibitors for advice. The breeder should have careful records on each rabbit, giving its pedigree and its mothers and fathers production record.

Housing

Rabbits are typically raised in cages as opposed to pens or loose in buildings. The cages can either be single-tier or double-tier. Single-tier cages makes cleaning and observation easier. Double-tier cages are more economical, as you can keep twice as many rabbits under one roof. Cages should be constructed of 14-gauge welded wire with ½- by 1-inch mesh. Any mesh smaller than that will make cleaning difficult, as manure will not be able to fall through. If you have a double-tier cage, the upper tier of cages will need a sided-catch pan of stainless steel to catch manure.

Suggested Cage Sizes	
Small breed	2 ½ x 2 ½ ft.
Medium breed	2 ½ x 3 ft.
Large breed	2 ½ x 4 ft.

The cages should be placed in a well-ventilated building on ground with good drainage. They can be suspended from the ceiling, but supporting legs will lend more stability to the cages. The roof of the building should be insulated to reduce heat absorption in the summer and condensation in the winter. Heat is not usually needed in the winter unless rabbits kindle during sub-zero weather. If you plan to have cages facing each other, you should have an aisle with a minimum width of three feet. Allow a generous space at the end of the aisle to be able to turn around a wheelbarrow or cart, which you will need to clean the rabbit manure.

Lighting should also be provided for 16 hours a day to help prevent breeding problems in the fall and winter — 25-watt lights are sufficient. There are many styles and varieties of waterers and feeders available for rabbits. A bottle waterer that attaches to the outside of the cage along with a metal feeder with an outside feed chute makes feeding and watering easy, as individual cage doors do not need to be opened. After rabbits are 3 months old, they should be segregated by sex, allowing two to a cage. After 5 months of age, each rabbit should have its own cage. This will prevent fighting and give each rabbit its own private area.

Handling

You should never pick a rabbit up by the ears. This can hurt their ears, and they will kick, potentially injuring their backs. Instead, gently slide one hand under its chest and the other underneath its rump. Lift the rabbit by lifting it up with the hand under the chest while scooping with the hand under the rump. Pull the rabbit toward your body and slide the rabbit along the arm, supporting its chest. Gently press the rabbit against your body, much like a football is held, with the arm supporting the body and the head tucked under the elbow. Try to handle your rabbits frequently, at least two to three times a week, so they get used to being held and also to check their health. Their back feet are very powerful, and if they feel frightened or insecure in your grasp, they will kick. This struggling can injure their backs, leading to paralysis or death.

Sexing

To determine the sex of a rabbit, you need to turn the rabbit on its back. Small rabbits can be turned on their back using the crook of your arm to hold them. For larger rabbits, sit down and turn them on their back in your lap. If the rabbit struggles, hold it securely until it stays still. Use one hand to hold the rabbit's chest and with the other, take your thumb and forefinger to part the hair near the tail to expose its genitals — the opening nearest the belly. The anus is closest to the tail. Adult males older than 20 weeks will have flesh-colored testicles lying near the genital openings. These may be covered by fur, so you may have to part the fur to find the testicles. If you do not see the testicles, you will need to place your thumb and your index finger on either side of the genital opening. Apply gentle pressure to expose the genitals. If you see a tube-like structure with a small opening, this is the penis. Females will also have a somewhat prominent structure, but instead of a small opening, there will be a slit-like opening.

Feeding

The best food for rabbits is a commercial rabbit pellet. This food is a complete feed, so use of supplemental salt or other feeds is not needed with pellets. Try to purchase only enough pellets that you can use in one month, and check the bags for a recent production date when you purchase the pellets. This way you will keep your feed supply as fresh as possible, as certain vitamins and some fats can deteriorate quickly after production.

Rabbits prefer to eat at night, so a good time to feed your rabbits is in the evening. Check the feeders daily for any wet or moldy feed. Empty as needed before refilling the feeders. The biggest health problem a rabbit has is overfeeding. Large breed rabbits need 4 to 6 ounces of pellets once a day. Small rabbits (dwarf type) need only 2 ounces of pellets a day. Rabbits should have access to good, leafy alfalfa hay at all times. The hay should be checked often to make sure it does not become moldy. A pregnant or lactating doe should have all the feed she wants. While her young are still with her (up to 8 weeks), they should all have free-choice feed along with plenty of water. If young bucks or does are being raised as breeding rabbits, they should be fed 1 ounce of feed daily for each pound of body weight.

Reproduction

Rabbits reach sexual maturity at different ages, depending on their size. A small breed, such as a Netherland Dwarf, will be able to be bred at 4 months old. A medium-sized rabbit like the Angoras will be able to be first bred at 5 to 6 months, and large breeds such as the Flemish Giant can be bred from 9 to 12 months of age. Most rabbits are bred through the natural breeding method. You should watch the doe for signs she is ready to be mated. These signs include:

- Restlessness and nervousness
- A deep red coloration of the vulva
- Rubbing her chin on equipment
- A desire to join other rabbits

You will want to keep two bucks for every ten to 20 does. If you have fewer than ten does, it is also wise to keep two bucks in case one buck fails to inseminate the does. Good bucks will have a productive mating life of two to four years. Bucks will molt (shed part of its fur coat) once a year for about a month and may not breed during this time period. The productive reproduction timeframe of a doe is two to three years. Do not breed closely related bucks and does such as siblings or half-siblings, as inbreeding will increase the chance of genetic defects.

The doe should always be brought to the buck's cage for mating; otherwise, she may fight him. When the mating is over, the doe should be removed from the buck's cage and returned to her cage. You will know the mating has been completed when the buck falls away to the side from the doe. If you do not see this motion, take the doe out of the pen and place her with another buck. The doe will ovulate about 12 hours after this first mating. The doe can be taken back for a second mating with the same buck at this time to help conception rates. If the doe tries to fight the buck, take her out right away and wait a few days before trying to mate her again. Once in while, you will encounter a female who is showing all the signs of being ready to mate but will not allow the buck to mate her. These does will need to be restrained so the buck can mount her, but this trait can be inherited, so it is best to get rid of these does so this trait is not passed on to her female progeny.

If you are breeding the rabbits for commercial meat production, a good breeding program to follow is to breed the does 42 days after kindling. This will let each doe produce five litters a year. With an average litter size of eight kits (newborn rabbits), this means each doe will produce 40 young rabbits each year. Keep records for each doe and buck during the breeding, including the pairs mated, date, and number of young kindled and weaned. This will help you keep track of productivity of each animal, and help you decide which rabbits to cull (get rid of) according to poor performance — fewer than seven young kindled per doe, or if bucks fail to service the does — or you can keep the young of those breeding pairs who perform exceptionally well.

Nest boxes

Nest boxes are necessary for the doe to kindle in so she has privacy and so the young are not born onto metal wire, which is too cold and can kill the newborns. These boxes can be built of any type of lumber, but a common box is built of plywood. The edges of the wood should be lined with galvanized metal, as the does will chew on the wood. A good box for a medium-sized rabbit is 18 by 10 by 8 inches. The top can be covered to provide extra privacy for the doe. You should place clean, dry bedding in the nest box, even though the doe will pluck her own fur to make a nest. This is especially important if the doe is kindling during cold weather. Soft grass, hay, wood shavings, or straw can all be used. The doe may eat some of the bedding, so replenish often. Place nest boxes into the pregnant doe's cage 27 days after breeding so she can get use to it.

Kindling

A doe will kindle around 31 days after she is bred. It is very important not to disturb a doe giving birth because she may then kill the young and eat them. You do want to observe her quietly from a distance to make sure she is giving birth. The day after kindling, you can check the nest box for any dead kits and take them away. Newborn rabbits are born with closed eyes and ears and are basically furless. The kits' eyes will open at around 10 days of age, and at 3 weeks they will begin to venture out of the nest box. They will begin to nibble on pellets and start to sip water, so keep feeders and waterers full of fresh material at all times.

Young rabbits will be ready to wean at 8 weeks of age, which is also the time when they can be marketed as live young or fryers.

If you happen to find that the kits are born outside the nest box, place them inside the box and cover them with the doe's fur that she has lined the nest with. Wait a couple of hours, and if the doe has not joined them inside the box, place her inside with them. Hold her inside until the kits start to nurse. Kits nurse once or twice a day for only two to four minutes. If a doe has more than eight kits, you can transfer some of the kits to another mother with fewer kits, as long as the young are around the same age. This will ensure there is enough milk to go around. Most does will accept the young of another mother without any problem.

Health

Good nutrition, sound breeding stock, regular cleaning and disinfecting of cages, feeders, and waterers, and weekly manure removal will go a long way to ensure your rabbits will remain in optimal health. Keeping your rabbit housing in good repair and well-ventilated are also part of keeping rabbits as healthy as they can be. The building and feed supply should be rodent-, predator-, and bird-proof. Cages and feeding and watering equipment should be disinfected on a regular basis. Nest boxes should also be disinfected after each litter and prior to placing into the expectant does in the cage. All manure and debris should be scraped from the item being disinfected before being scrubbed with a disinfecting solution. Bleach water, vinegar, or a commercial disinfectant can be used. After disinfecting, the item should be allowed to dry thoroughly before being placed into use. Letting the item dry in the sunlight lends an additional level of sanitation.

Despite all this attention, occasionally you may have some health problems crop up in your rabbits. To minimize losses, you should daily observe all your rabbits. Are they eating their feed and drinking their water? Does the manure under the pen appear normal? Are their eyes clear and noses free from discharge? Do they act interested in your presence at the front of their cage? Many diseases are hard to detect with just a brief visual observation. You should closely examine your rabbits at least once a week by handling them and checking their ears, toenails, and teeth. The ears should be clean and dry. The toenails should not be overly long. The teeth should not be long or cutting into the roof of the mouth.

Common health problems include ear mange, coccidiosis, and pasteurellosis. Many diseases are spread through the introduction of new animals into an established herd. New animals should be quarantined from the main herd for 14 days and observed for any sign of disease during this time period. If you do find a sick animal, either a new arrival or one from your establish herd, the sick rabbit should be isolated from the rest of the rabbits, preferably in a different building. The sick animal should only be cared for after you have taken care of the healthy rabbits. Wash your hands and disinfect your shoes after caring for the sick animals. If the rabbit dies, its carcass should be burned or buried to stop the spread of diseases. Any pens and equipment used for caring for the sick rabbit should be cleaned and disinfected before being reused.

Pasteurellosis: This disease is caused by the bacterium *Pasteurella multocida*. Pasteurellosis causes many different types of infections including snuffles (rhinitis), abscesses, pneumonia, pyometra (uterine infection), ear infections, and eye infections. This is a fairly common disease of the nasal sinuses. The rabbit has trouble breathing due to a thick discharge from the nose and makes a characteristic nasal sound when trying to breath. The front paws may become wet with the discharge as it tries to clean its nose. The rabbit can spread the disease through sneezing, and objects used in its cage become loaded with the microorganism. It is difficult to eradicate the bacteria from the infected rabbits, although antibiotics can be used in pet or show animals. If the rabbits are used for meat, it is not advised to give them antibiotics, as it can remain in the meat for some time after administration; this is an illegal practice in most states. Penicillin is not to be used in rabbits, as it can cause a fatal toxemia in this species. Rabbits affected with pasteurellosis in a commercial enterprise should be culled and their carcasses burned or buried to prevent the spread of the disease. All equipment and cages contacted by the sick rabbit should be thoroughly disinfected.

Enterotoxemia: This disease is characterized by an explosive diarrhea. It usually occurs in young rabbits 1 to 2 months old. The rabbits may be normal one day, then found dead the next. It is caused by a bacterium, *Clostridium spiroforme*, which releases a deadly toxin causing death in one to two days after infection. How the rabbits are infected with these bacteria is not entirely known, but it is thought that giving rabbits extra fiber such as supplemental hay will help reduce the disease occurrence. Giving rabbits penicillin will also cause enterotoxemia.

Coccidiosis: This disease is caused by a protozoa parasite. Coccidiosis affects the liver and intestine of rabbits causing diarrhea, loss of appetite, and weight loss. Occasionally a rabbit will die from coccidiosis. It is spread through fecal contamination of cages, waterers, and feeders, so daily cleaning of these items will help reduce the incidence of coccidiosis. Treatment is through feeding a medicated feed for two to three weeks to reduce the number of parasites.

Torticollis (wry neck): Wry neck occurs when otitis media (inflammation of the middle ear) spreads to the inner ear. The inner ear regulates an animal's equilibrium, so when it is infected or damaged, it causes the head to tilt. An inner ear infection is very hard to treat, as antibiotics have difficulty penetrating this area of the body. Rabbits that do recover from an inner ear infection may have a permanent head tilt.

Ear mites: Ear mites are the most common external parasite of rabbits. Mites invade the ear and thick, brown crusts of serum accumulate inside the ear. The rabbit shakes its head and scratches its ears due to the intense itching. When the rabbit tries to scratch the itch, the toenails on the hind feet cause scratches to the outside of the ear, as well. Serious infections can cause weight loss, nerve damage, and ear infection due to bacterial invasion. Even if only one rabbit in your herd is showing signs of an ear mite infection, all rabbits should be treated because it is easy for the mites to pass from rabbit to rabbit. If there is a lot of debris built up in the ear, mineral oil should be placed in the ear to soften the debris. The material should then be wiped out with a cotton ball. Medication is readily available in the form of eardrops, which you can pick up at your local veterinarian's office. Each ear should be treated and the base of the ear massaged after applying the drug.

Hutch burn: This is a condition caused by rabbits being subjected to wet and dirty floors. The anus and genital region of the rabbit become chapped and red. The damp condition irritates these delicate membranes, and soon they become infected with a secondary bacterial infection. There is no reason for this condition to occur if you keep your pens clean and dry. Treatment is cleaning and drying the pen, and application of antibiotic ointment to the affected areas.

Fungal infections: Rabbits can harbor fungus that cause skin lesions. These fungi can also be transmitted by and to humans. A rabbit with a fungal infection will have patchy hair loss, usually around the nose, eyelids, ears, and face. The affected skin may also become thickened and have yellow crusts. Usually the young rabbit will show more severe hair loss and skin changes. Treatment consists of spot treatment of affected areas with an antifungal ointment. If many rabbits are affected, oral medication can be given.

External parasites (fleas, mites): Rabbits generally have mites on their skin, which usually does not become a problem unless the animal becomes unhealthy. Then the mites can flourish, causing intense itching, hair loss, and sores. To treat external parasites, apply a cat flea powder weekly. This treatment is also effective against the rabbit flea, a very seldom-encountered parasite in domestic rabbits. If your rabbit does have fleas, its environment will also need to be treated with an insecticide to destroy flea eggs and larva.

Conjunctivitis (pink eye): Young rabbits are commonly affected by conjunctivitis, especially those that are raised in crowded conditions. Bacteria invade the conjunctiva (the red lining around the eye) and cause infection. The eye then becomes red and swollen. A thick discharge collects around the eye, frequently pasting the eye shut. One or both eyes may be affected. Treatment is by gently washing the eyelid with a warm washcloth to remove the discharge, flushing the eye with sterile saline, and treating the eyes with an eye antibiotic ointment.

Pododermatitis: This condition comes with ulcers or sores on the feet or footpads. It is usually associated with rabbits kept on wire-floored cages. To treat, place a flat piece of wood on the floor of the cage, cleaning it frequently if it becomes dirty. Using straw bedding can help alleviate the condition as well. Sores or ulcers can be treated with protective ointments you can obtain from your local veterinarian's office.

Urolithiasis: Rabbits excrete calcium in their urine, giving the urine a cloudy appearance. Because of this excretion, they are prone to urine calcium sludge or stone formation. Feeding rabbits an excessive amount of calcium (as can be found in alfalfa hay) or genetics can predispose a rabbit to this disease. A rabbit affected by urolithiasis will strain when trying to urinate, will go off feed, and have a painful abdomen and bloody urine. To prevent this from occurring, feed your rabbits grass hay and make sure they have plenty of water at all time.

Malocclusion: A rabbit's teeth continuously grow throughout its lifetime, and they should be straight and meet evenly. If the teeth do not meet properly, this condition is called malocclusion. This can become a serious issue, as overgrown teeth will lead to the rabbit's not being able to eat properly, or to mouth and jaw problems. A rabbit with this condition will need to have its teeth regularly trimmed by a veterinarian. Hay in the diet seems to help lessen the occurrence of teeth overgrowing.

Pregnancy-related problems

Mastitis: Does can acquire mastitis, or an infection of the mammary glands, while producing milk. The glands become swollen, hot, and reddened or bluish, and milk production may cease. Bacteria enter the mammary glands and invade the tissues. The most common bacteria causing mastitis is *Staphylococcus aureus*, a bacterium found in the nasal passages of all rabbits. The affected doe usually stops eating and may refuse to nurse her kits. The kits can also become infected through drinking infected milk. Treatment is through use of antibiotics and good nursing care. The kits born of a doe with mastitis should be hand-fed; do not foster them to another doe, as this can spread the disease to the doe and her young.

False pregnancy: Does can sometimes exhibit a false pregnancy. This can occur due to mating with a buck that does not result in pregnancy or by being mounted by another doe. Even though the doe does not conceive, she will go through all the pregnancy-related hormonal changes. The false pregnancy will last 16 to 18 days. At the end, the doe may build a nest and may even produce milk. She will eventually return to normal and be able to breed again.

Pregnancy toxemia: Does in the last few days of pregnancy or during the first few days after birth are susceptible to this condition. It is a fairly common condition, but very little is known about how it occurs. Does stop eating, become depressed and weak, abort the kits, and can die. The liver becomes infiltrated with fat and enlarges. This stops the normal functioning of the liver. One major function of the liver is to remove toxins from the blood. Treatment consists of force-feeding the doe and use of steroids, which are only available from a veterinarian. Obese does or does with hairballs from nest building are most susceptible to pregnancy toxemia.

CASE STUDY: THOSE SILLY RABBITS

Scott Marshall
Marshall Farms
9212 Neal Avenue South
Hastings, Minnesota
marshallrabbits@yahoo.com

Scott Marshall started raising rabbits at a young age. His parents were hog and grain farmers, and he received four or five pet rabbits when he was about 10. Now, he raises about 150 rabbits, and it is definitely a family project. His 11-year-old daughter, Rebecca, helps care for the rabbits with supervision. Marshall definitely thinks rabbits are a good family project. It helps children learn a lot of life lessons: how to care for animals; how to follow the rules; and the fact that animals die.

Marshall recommends that a person interested in raising rabbits does the homework first. Think about the worst part of the year — typically winter. A rabbit grower needs to be out there every day, in all kinds of weather, to feed and water the rabbits twice a day. Another useful piece of advice is to find a market and local processer if you do not want to process them yourself early in the process.

Marshall spends five hours a day on the weekdays, and four to eight hours a day on weekends caring for his rabbits. Much of his time is spent on his three tasks: cleaning the barn and cages, butchering and packaging rabbit meat, and feeding and watering the rabbits. Cold winter weather makes his work more difficult when he has to thaw out water cups and tackle frozen manure. Predators can be a real problem as well: Stray dogs, raccoons, possums, cats, and coyotes can kill adult rabbits. Rats can kill young bunnies. Bees and wasp stings can also kill a rabbit. Marshall counters these dangers by having a barn with a strong door and a lock.

As for health problems, Marshall has some great advice for the beginning farmer: "Clean, clean, clean, and protect," he said. "What I mean is clean water, clean feed, clean housing and nests boxes, and protect from weather and predators. That will take care of most of the health issues. In my 30 years raising rabbits, I have been lucky not to have had any major issues."

Marshall also had to deal with sore feet, colds, and ear mites, "That was my fault for bringing in new stock and not quarantining them," he said. "Quarantining new stock is very important. Also, don't be a petting zoo. Sick people can make sick rabbits. It also stresses the rabbits. And that weed a kid pulls to feed the bunny could be poisonous."

The Marshalls take great satisfaction in knowing they provide their family and customers with healthy, quality meat, and they enjoy raising rabbits. Marshall is optimistic about the future market for rabbits. He loves the renewed interest in eating locally. "It's back to the basics — the way our grandparents and their parents ate," he said.

CHAPTER 6

The Curious Goat

The goat was probably one of the first domesticated animals, providing people with milk, meat, and clothing. These versatile, agile animals descended from mountain goats in Western Asia. The domestic goat *(Capra hircus)* descended from the wild goat *(Capra aegagrus)* from central Asia. They are also closely related to sheep. Goats are a fairly easy-to-keep species because they have minimal housing needs. They also eat very little grain, but they do need good quality hay and pasture. One big advantage of owning goats is that they will eat many weeds and brush that cattle will not consume. However, contrary to popular belief, goats will not eat tin cans or garbage. Such items may actually prove to be a health hazard to goats, and they should not be given access to these non-food items.

Goats are very curious animals, and they love to explore their environment with their lips and tongues. They are also very smart and will search fences, gates, gate latches, and their living quarters for an escape route from confinement. Because of their nimbleness and good sense of balance, they are high climbers and can even climb over fences. Low tree limbs surrounding pens or pastures also provide another escape route for goats.

Goats are a versatile breed in terms of providing humans with food and fiber. Their meat is popular around the world, and the Boer goat is a popular meat goat. Dairy goats provide milk, which can be substituted for cow's milk for people with allergies. Goat's milk is made into cheese, butter, yogurt, and ice cream. Unlike cow's milk, goat's milk is naturally homogenized, and the fat stays suspended in the fluid — goat milk has a slightly sweet taste. In terms of fiber, the Angora goats give plenty of mohair, up to 15 pounds yearly, to be woven into fine clothing articles. Likewise, each mature Cashmere goat yields about 9 ounces of soft cashmere wool each year.

Breeds

Before you decide on a breed of goat, you will want to determine what you want to achieve with your goats. Are you primarily interested in goats for milk? Do you want to raise goats for meat? Some breeds of goats are better suited for meat production, and others are high milk-producing goats. Goat breeds vary with weight and size. This is important when considering your pasture availability — smaller goats will take less pasture to maintain weight. However, you might sacrifice on meat quantities with a smaller goat. Smaller dairy goats might also give less milk, but if the goat milk is strictly for family consumption, this might be a good option for you. There are more than 300 different breeds of goats in the world. To get you started, the following is a brief introduction to the breeds and types of goats commonly raised in North America. Some breeds may not be available in your area, so you will need to do some sleuthing to find out if the specific breeders are near you — not all breeds are raised in every country. Your local county extension agent can help you locate goat farms in your area.

Alpine: The Alpine goat was developed in Switzerland. Its ears are upright, and the face is dished or scooped. The Alpine is usually brown and white or black and white, although other colors are also seen. It is primarily used as a dairy goat. Females weigh about 135 pounds, and males weigh around 170 pounds.

Angora: The Angora goat is used as a fiber goat for its mohair fleece. On average, more than 10 pounds of mohair are sheared from the average Angora goat. Mohair is similar in chemical composition to wool but has a smoother surface, giving it a silky texture. Angora goats of both sexes have horns and droopy ears. Does usually weigh 80 pounds as adults. Bucks average 200 pounds. As an added bonus, Angora goats are fantastic browsers, controlling weeds and brush in areas inaccessible to mowers.

Boer: The Boer goat has pendulous ears. It was developed in South Africa as a meat goat and gains around a quarter pound of weight daily until it reaches full maturity. This is the best-performing goat in terms of weight gain among the meat-type goats, making the Boer goat reaches market weigh very quickly. The doe will commonly have twins. Males weigh around 260 pounds when mature, while females weigh around 215 pounds.

LaMancha: The LaMancha is quickly recognized by its very small ears. It was developed in the United States from crossing Spanish goats with Swiss and Nubian bucks. It is an excellent dairy goat, giving milk with high butterfat. The LaMancha goat can come in a variety of colors and has a calm and gentle temperament.

Nubian: The Nubian goat is a large animal with a convex nose and long, pendulous ears. It is the most common breed and makes a good dairy goat, producing milk that is high in butterfat, but it does produce less milk per day than other dairy goat breeds. It also produces a fair amount of meat and is considered a dual-purpose goat breed. The does generally weigh at least 135 pounds when mature, and the buck weighs at least 175 pounds at maturity. The Nubian is usually brown.

Oberhasli: This breed is typically a deep, reddish brown with black stripes on the face. The breed was developed in Switzerland and was formerly known as the Swiss Alpine. This breed is slightly smaller than other standard-sized goat breeds, but is a good dairy goat breed, giving up to 1 ½ gallons of milk per day. The breed is considered to be a fairly rare breed but is growing in popularity.

Pygmy: The Pygmy goat comes from Africa and is primarily kept as a pet. The Pygmy goat has a straight, medium-long hair coat, and it may be of any color. It has a small, blocky body. Does should measure less than 22 ⅜ inches at the withers, while bucks should measure less than 23 ⅜ at the top of the shoulders.

Saanen goat

Saanen: This breed is usually all white. The Saanen was developed in Switzerland but quickly spread throughout Europe. The does are heavy milkers and weigh about 145 pounds. They are also the largest of the dairy goat breeds.

Toggenburg: Another Swiss breed, the Toggenburg is mid-sized and rich brown with white highlights. The hair is short to medium in length, and they are a solid color from light fawn to dark brown. They also have white markings on the legs and two white stripes down the face. They are a dairy goat breed, and does give up to 1 ½ gallons of milk per day.

Housing

The goat shelter should protect the goat from wind, predators, and wet weather. Your geographical location will drive your housing scheme for goats. In dry, arid regions, little will be needed other than wind and shade protection. Colder, harsher climates will require a more sturdy structure to protect the goats from winter wind chill and wet snow. If you plan on having dairy goats, your housing plans will need to be a bit more elaborate. The barn should be a sturdy structure devoted to your dairy herd and should not house other goats or animals. Pens do not need to be cemented but should be maintained in a clean and dry manner. The does can be kept in a loose housing situation, which provides one or two large pens for the goats, or the does can be confined to their own individual pen or tie-stall.

Each type of housing presents its own benefits and problems. A loose house situation gives the does exercise and social contact. The manure pack can provide extra warmth in the winter as it emits some heat and insulates from the ground. The big disadvantage of a loose housing situation is it is hard to maintain the manure pack with a dry upper layer. Hay must be fed off the ground to lessen the transmission of parasites. The individual pen housing option will have higher initial costs due to pen or stall construction and can deprive the does of exercise and social contact. With the loose housing option, the does can also be provided with outside access to a pen or pasture during good weather. This is also the most popular option for young stock and meat-type goats. Bucks should also be given their own shelter with the same standard as the housing for the does and young stock.

The milking area for the does should be located away from the stable and needs to have a concrete floor. An 8-by-8-foot area will be sufficient for milking one or two does at a time. A drain should also be placed in the concrete to allow for thorough cleaning of the milking area. If your plans include selling the milk to the public, please check with your state milk board for the particular requirements for the milking area. It will need to pass state inspection before the milk can be sold. Of course, if your family is consuming the milk, you will still want to have a clean, pest-free milking area to ensure they consume quality milk. Does are trained to be milked on a milking platform, which is generally 18 inches by 3 ½ feet. They are mounted on stilt or legs to allow the platform to be 15 to 18 inches from the floor. This will help facilitate milking, and a trained goat will readily leap onto the stand, particularly if she fed her grain ration at this time.

Other necessary equipment in the milking area is a hot water heater, a double sink, a rack for drying and storing milking equipment, and a refrigeration source. You will need the hot water and sinks to clean and sanitize your milking equipment. A regular refrigerator can be used for family milk consumption. If you have a larger herd or plan to sell to the public or a milk processor, you will need to invest in a cooler or a bulk tank. The walls and ceilings should be free from drips and should not allow moisture to condense. To help combat moisture problems, adequate ventilation should be maintained. Insulation can also help prevent condensation from forming during periods of cold weather. Electricity to the building is a must to run exhaust fans and to provide light. The temperature in the dairy goat barn should be monitored. Temperatures above 80°F can negatively impact milk production, making the does uncomfortable and stressed. A stressed doe will not be able to give as much milk as a comfortable goat. Again, adequate ventilation through air movement can help keep the temperature cool. Ventilation can be provided through open windows, use of exhaust fans, and through use of large, industrial-sized barn fans.

Goats can and will wiggle through the smallest of holes just for the fun of it, so fences should not only keep predators out, but also keep goats in. Two types of fencing can be used. The first consists of a 4-foot, woven-wire fence. A 14-gauge strand of electrical fence wire should be strung 12 inches from the top of the wire. This wire should be electrified with a charger. Sturdy corner posts will need to be properly placed before the wire is strung. Posts can either be steel or wood and should be spaced every 12 feet to provide support for the fence material. The other option is to use an entirely electrical fence. The first wire is place 12 inches from the ground, followed by four more wires spaced 6 inches apart. Insulators will always be needed with electrical wires to keep them from shorting out, and brush and weeds will need to be controlled along the fence line. This type of fencing is suited for either corrals or a pasture situation. Periodically, test your fences to make sure chargers are working properly, and walk the fence line at least once per week to check for damage. If you do not, you can be certain your goats will immediately zone in on any trouble spots and escape from your pen.

Feeding

A little grain, a little hay, and a little grass: That is all a goat really needs, right? Well, they do need those things — but also a few others in order to provide you with healthy goats that gain weight efficiently and produce milk. They also need a few supplemental items to maintain their health.

The basic idea behind feeding goats is to feed growing goats enough energy in the form of grain to allow them to grow and to feed the mature goat enough energy to maintain their body weight. In addition, a pregnant or lactating doe will need to be given a little extra energy to feed her developing fetus or to produce enough milk to feed her young. Dairy goats in full milk production will also need extra grain. Grain and hay should be fed in hayracks and troughs. If you are feeding dairy goats, ideally each goat will have a spot to feed separately to make sure each doe gets her needed grain. All feeders should be designed so that the goats are unable to jump into the hay or grain. There are many styles of hay and grain feeders available. A popular model has a keyhole design, which allows the goat to stick its head in it and feed but is unable to pull out measurable amounts of hay or grain.

Forage

A major part of a goat's diet is forage; this is pasture or hay. It is more cost-effective and better for the goat's overall health to feed it on primarily forage. Hay should be high-quality grass or legume

Photo provided by Jason and Karlia Dahl

hay that is free of molds and weeds. Goats are picky hay eaters and will consume only the most palatable portions of hay.

Good hay will have plenty of leafy material and minimal stems. It should smell sweet and not earthy or moldy. Moldy or musty-smelling hay may indicate the hay was put up wet — a sure path to a spoiled batch of hay. It should also have a slight green tinge to the majority of the hay bale. However, simply eyeballing your hay supply will not guarantee the hay is top quality. The relative feed value (RFV) is a test performed on hay samples, which can tell you how much of the hay ruminants can use: the higher the value, the higher the quality of hay. Generally, hay with legumes like alfalfa or clover will have a higher percentage of protein than hay made from grasses. This type of hay will have a higher RFV but will also cost more than lesser RFV value hay. Mature goats can generally be fed a lesser RFV value hay than milking or pregnant does.

Pasturing goats during the pasture season is generally the most cost-effective way to feed goats. Aside from pregnant or lactating goats, or meat goats being fed up for slaughter, goats on good, growing pastures will not need supplemental grain. Pastures should be planted with a premium pasture mix or a good blend of grasses and legumes. Goat pastures should also be well-drained to make the pasture more inhospitable to certain internal parasites of goats. Rotating pastures will help you to maximize the use of the pastures and help break disease cycles. Plan to divide your pasture into at least six paddocks of at least one acre each. One acre can support up to eight adult goats. The ultimate size of the paddocks will depend on how big your herd is and the size of the goats. Goats are different from cattle in their grazing patterns. Goats prefer to nibble on the leaves and tender shoots of grass nearer the ground then cattle.

Because of goats' particular eating habits, they are very susceptible to the spread on intestinal parasites. Many of the internal parasites are spread through fecal contamination of pasture. The lower to the ground the animal grazes, the bigger the chance of becoming infected. Therefore, it is imperative that a pasture rotation for goats considers this susceptibility for disease transmission. Allowing three weeks (which is generally the life cycle of some dangerous goat parasites) between grazing a particular pasture will allow the number of parasites on the pasture to decrease. Stock your paddocks lightly until you are able to ascertain how many goats one paddock can reasonably hold. This means by the end of the rotation of a particular pasture, the grass should look grazed but not look like a lawn mower went over it.

One of the main reasons people purchase goats is to remove weed or overgrowth in wooded or hard-to-mow areas. Goats are nimble and are able to graze ground that cattle would not be able to reach. In addition, goats enjoy nibbling at brush and the lower leaves of trees in their quest for tasty new growth. They can eat many weeds, such as poison ivy, sumac, and briar, without any ill effects. If you do use your goats to clear brush or weeds, keep in mind they will not eat every weed unless they are forced to do so. They will not gain weight as readily as on a pasture diet, and they may even lose weight, but your weeds will be controlled.

Grain

Grain formulated for cattle can be fed to goats if you are unable to find a goat grain ration at your local grain elevator or feed store. If you do need to purchase cattle feed, do not feed grain with added urea, as goats do not like the taste and may waste the grain. If you are feeding a milking herd, the level of protein in the grain should be 15 percent if your hay is made of mostly legumes. Mineral mix should be a high phosphorus mix. If your hay is mostly grass, the grain protein level should be around 17 percent, and mineral supplement should be a 2:1 calcium and phosphorus ratio. If your dairy goats are thin, hay should always be available for them, and grain should be heavily supplemented. Feed 1 pound of grain per every 3 to 4 pounds of milk produced.

Dry does (those does that are not milking) can be fed all the hay or pasture they want, along with ½ to 1 pound of grain daily. Two weeks prior to kidding, the doe should be switched back to a milking grain diet. Bucks should be fed grain at the rate of 1 pound of grain daily, plus hay or pasture. You do not want them to get fat, so if this happens, cut back on the grain. Kids that are nursing should be allowed to nibble on grain to get them used to this new food source. Around weaning time (when the kids are 2 to 3 months of age), allow 1 to 2 pounds of grain daily per kid. Goats being raised for meat should be fed ¼ to 1 pound of grain daily, depending on forage quality. Goats on a productive pasture can be fed a lesser amount. You should feed the goat more grain if its diet source is only hay.

All told the above feeding guidelines are just that: guidelines. Use your own judgment and observations to gauge how much feed to give to your goats. When you switch feed sources or rations, be sure to do so gradually — typically over a week's time — so as not to upset the goat's digestive system.

Water

Water is the most important nutrient needed by goats. Your goats should always have access to clean, palatable water. Water can be fed in buckets, or a livestock water fountain can be installed to supply a continuous source of fresh water. If you water your goats via buckets, the supply should be refreshed daily and the bucket cleaned regularly. If the goats defect in the bucket or water fountain, it should be disinfected and thoroughly rinsed to prevent the spread of disease and parasites. In warm weather, cool but not ice cold water should be offered. In very hot weather, check your goats' water supply twice daily. In cold weather, warm water should be offered to encourage your goats to drink. If you experience freezing of your water supply, invest in a heated water bucket or a fountain heater to keep ice from forming. If you do not do this, at least check the water twice daily for freezing, and remove ice.

Supplements

Goats will need to be fed supplements in the form of trace minerals, salt, and soda. Soda, which is basically livestock-grade baking soda, is necessary to keep the rumen pH at an appropriate level. It is an alkaline substance that will help control the acid content in the rumen. Soda should be offered continuously to goats in a feeder. They will consume soda as needed to keep their stomachs at the proper pH. Goats also need salt and trace minerals — especially selenium, copper, and iodine — for proper body functioning. This can be purchased at a feed store in a loose form or in compressed blocks. Goats usually do better with the loose form, as during hot weather they cannot consume enough block salt to replace salt loss; salt blocks are very hard and have to be continuously licked. If your feed store does not sell mineral salt specifically for goats, get the mineral salt formulated for cattle or horses. Soda and mineral salt should be available in clean containers that are protected from moisture. They should be offered separately. There are many different types of salt and soda feeders available at affordable prices. The soda and mineral salt should be checked frequently and changed if it becomes caked or damp.

Using Goats for Weed Control

Photo provided by Jason and Karlia Dahl

As stated earlier, goats can and are used to control weeds. This type of use is called managed defoliation in an attempt to reduce unwanted shrubs and weeds in an area while increasing the numbers of wanted

grasses. Results are evident after one year of grazing, but it typically takes up to four years to get good brush control. Grazing while brush and weeds are rapidly growing, typically in the spring and summer, is more effective than trying to start a brush control program after the weeds are mature, as the goats will not be consume as much of the mature plants as the young plants.

Using goats to control saplings, brush, and weeds in wooded areas has also been practiced. It has been found that goats prefer to graze on vines and poison ivy instead of tree leaves. This can be a great way to clear out an old, overgrown woody area in an environmentally sound manner. Whether the goats are clearing an old pasture, a rocky hillside, or grove of trees, fencing must be maintained, and predator control will need to be closely monitored. It might be best to have the goats brought in closer to home from the grazing area if coyotes or other predators are a problem. Goats should be kept on the area you want grazed until the majority of the weeds or brushed are consumed.

Reproduction

A doe will reach puberty between 7 to 10 months of age, and a buck will be ready to breed at 8 to 10 months of age. One buck can breed 20 to 30 does. Generally, an older buck can service more does than a younger buck. Two or three weeks before you plan to breed your goats, you should deworm the herd and trim their hooves. The does should also be vaccinated with a clostridium perfringens (type C and D), plus tetanus toxoid vaccine at this time. Another dose will need to be given four to six weeks prior to the anticipated kidding date. This will give the kids immunity to these two serious diseases.

Goats are seasonal breeders, meaning they have a certain time period that they bred. In the United States, they will generally breed in the late fall to early winter and kid in the spring. Does are influenced by the scent of a buck to come into heat, usually about seven to ten days after exposure to a buck. Does in heat are very vocal, bleating loudly, almost as if they are in pain or very hungry. Other signs of heat in a doe include tail wagging; a swollen, reddened vulva; and frequent urination. The buck should be kept with the does for two heat cycles (42 days). This time period will make certain all does capable of being bred are actually bred.

Kidding

Does have a gestation period of 146 to 155 days. A few days prior to the expected due day, the doe should be moved to a pen that is clean, dry, and well-bedded. Feeding a pregnant doe hay or grain at night tends to delay birthing until early morning. A doe will start to develop an udder a few weeks to a couple of days prior to giving birth. It becomes tight and may appear glossy. Other signs kidding is about to start include a flabby vulva and vulvar discharge.

A doe goes through three stages of labor. During the first stage, the doe becomes restless, paws at the bedding, may look or nip at her sides, and may become very vocal. This stage can last from a few hours up to 24 hours. The second stage of labor is the actual birthing process. The doe may lie down and stand up numerous times as she goes into labor. Most does will kid just fine without assistance, but occasionally there will be problems. The kid should come front–feet first with the head between the legs. After the kid is delivered, the doe will clean the kid and dry it off. It is a good practice to dip the newborn's navel in a 7 percent tincture of iodine to prevent a naval infection. Stage three of labor is the delivery of the placenta, or afterbirth. This may take a few hours to pass. Once the doe passes it, remove it from the pen and discard it in the garbage.

Newborn

The newborn goat will need colostrum from its mother in order to build its immune system. Colostrum is the first milk the doe produces and is rich in vital antibodies to develop the kid's immune system. If the mother is unable to nurse the kid or if you have doubts that it received its first colostrum, milk the doe until you collect a half of a cup of colostrum. Feed this to the kid and carefully watch it nurse during the first few days of life. If you determine you need to hand-feed the kid, milk the doe and store the milk in the refrigerator to feed the kid. If the mother does not have milk, a milk replacer can be fed. Feed or farm supply stores carry milk replacer. It should have at least 20 percent fat and 20 percent protein derived from milk products.

A newborn kid up to 3 days old should be fed ½ cup of milk or milk replacer four to five times daily. From 4 days to 2 weeks old, the amount fed should be increased to 1 to 1 ½ cup milk three to four times daily. From 2 weeks to 3 months old, the kid can be fed 2 cups milk two or three times a day. Starting at one week of age, hay and grain can be provided for the kid to nibble. This will help its rumen mature. The rumen is a part of the goat's stomach in which many microorganisms are present to help digest the plant material a goat eats. Baby goats need time to develop this part of the stomach into a functioning rumen before it can use plants or hay as a food source. Always keep fresh and clean water available for the kid. When the kid is eating ¼ pound of grain daily and helping itself to hay, it can be weaned from milk. This usually happens when the kid is 2 to 3 months of age.

Health

One of the common problems of goat is foot rot. This disease is caused by a mixed infection with two bacteria and is exacerbated by wet soils and goats standing in manure. Usually the disease starts as an inflammation of the skin between the toes and then spreads to the hooves, causing pain and lameness. Careful, regular inspection of your goat's feet will catch the problem early and keep a mild infection from permanently damaging the goat's feet.

Feet should be kept trimmed to keep any hoof overgrowth from trapping dirt or manure — a perfect environment for the hoof rot bacteria to grow. You will need a hoof pick, hoof knife, and hoof shears to trim the feet. The goat should be restrained by using a halter to tie the goat to a post, and a person should hold the goat steady while another person works on the feet. The hoof should be picked up, and any manure, dirt, or stones should be removed using the hoof pick. If the wall of the hoof (the outer edge) is curled over the sole (the bottom of the foot), it should be removed using hoof shears.

Any excess growth on the toe should be trimmed off as well. Next, the hoof knife is used to trim off thin slices of the sole and heel until the bottom of the foot is trimmed to a flat surface. If you begin to see pink tissue, stop. This is the quick, and the foot will start to bleed if you go any deeper than this layer. When finished, the bottom of the foot should be flat on the ground, with the hoof forming a 45-degree angle with the ground.

If the goat has foot rot, all hoof equipment used should be cleaned and disinfected after use. Treat the affected feet with an antibiotic spray or other foot rot treatments. Keep the affected animal off muddy or damp ground for two weeks to allow the feet to heal. If you have a herd-wide problem, there are footbaths available, which can be filled with solutions such as formalin or zinc sulfate. All the animals in the herd should be forced to walk through the solution.

Other diseases

Haemonchus contortus (barber pole worm): This is a blood-sucking stomach worm, which causes severe anemia and death in goats and sheep. It can become a severe problem in warm, humid weather. The larva live on pasture grasses. Once it is eaten, it develops into adult worms in the stomach. The female worm can lay thousands of eggs a day and sucks blood from the stomach lining. The eggs pass through the feces and contaminate the goat's environment. Treatment is through use of dewormers. Prevention revolves around not overstocking pastures and rotating grazing of pastureland.

Meningeal deerworm: The white-tailed deer spreads this parasite. It usually does not cause problems in the deer, but when goats or sheep inadvertently ingest the worm larva, it damages the brain and spinal cord, frequently causing death. Some infected animals will have mild signs such as limping or leg weakness, while others become paralyzed. The disease cannot be diagnosed definitively in a live animal because the eggs do not show up in the feces, nor can the parasite be detected in a blood sample. Direct examination of the brain and spinal cord is necessary for a diagnosis. Diagnosis is based upon signs and health history. Treatment is through use of high doses of dewormer, along with supportive treatments such as steroids to reduce brain or spinal cord inflammation. Treatment will not reduce the damage done to the brain or spinal cord. To prevent, put up fencing to keep deer away.

Caseous lymphadenitis: This is a chronic bacterial infection of goats and sheep caused by *Corynebacterium pseudotuberculosis*. This bacterium enters the body through wounds, causing abscesses. Once the disease is in the herd, it can quickly spread to other animals. Treatment involves lancing the abscess, draining the abscess material into a bag or container, and cleaning out the abscess with a disinfecting solution. The abscess material should not be allowed to contaminate the pens, building, or soil, and it should be burned.

Enterotoxemia: *Clostridium perfringens* (type C and type D) cause this disease. Type C is primarily seen in young goats, causing bloody diarrhea or sudden death. Type D (also known as overeating disease) affects weaned goats that are being fed high amounts of grains or that have an abrupt switch from a no- or low-grain diet to a high-grain diet. Affected goats are usually found dead without other signs. Others will appear to have a severe case of painful diarrhea. Treatment is with an antitoxin and supportive care. Prevention is through vaccinating pregnant does prior to breeding and three to four weeks prior to delivery.

CASE STUDY:
DOWN ON THE GOAT FARM

Jason and Karlia Dahl
coyotepass@tnics.com
605-880-1354
Strandburg, South Dakota

Jason and Karlia Dahl's Boer goat farm on the South Dakota prairie is an ideal place to raise goats — and kids. They and their children have a farm well off the beaten path on a maze of gravel roads crisscrossing the gently rolling grassy plains. The Dahls decided to raise goats to help control the weeds on their new homestead, which has been allowed to revert back to nature after the former owners moved out.

They did their research and decided to purchase four goats — three does and a buck started their herd, which now numbers more than 70 of the brown and white Boer meat goats. They suggest that anyone interested in small-scale meat goat farming do their homework first, paying special attention to how to keep your goats healthy. The best advice they have is to talk to others in the business prior to purchasing any goats.

Raising goats is definitely a family project. The kids pitch in to help with the chores, as cleaning pens, trimming hooves, and vaccinations are big projects. Kidding season is the most time-consuming chore. Starting in late spring, they check the goats every two hours, day and night, to catch any does that might be having trouble giving birth. Their hard work pays off during the grazing season when they watch the young goats frolic on the grassy hills, which is the best part of goat farming in their opinion.

They have invested quite a bit of money and time into their goat operation. Fences are the biggest project. They need to be goat-proof, as goats are masters at escaping from even the best-planned fence. The Dahls use two strands of smooth, electric wire in the pasture, and in the barnyard, they use woven wire topped with barbed wire to keep escapes to a minimum. Housing needs for the goats are met using the existing buildings on the farm. The biggest need for housing is for small pens for the does when kidding; otherwise, the goats spend most of their time outside.

The Dahls market their goats both directly off the farm and through a sales barn. They sell both breeding goats and goats for meat. The children show goats at the county Achievement Days, and they hope to expand to other shows as well. The market for meat goats is fairly steady and is expected to grow somewhat in the future. In the meanwhile, the Dahls keep busy with their playful goats and take time to enjoy them each day.

CHAPTER 7

The Serene Sheep

A pasture full of white, wooly sheep with lambs bounding at their sides is a soothing image most people try to drift off to sleep to. It is hard to imagine a more serene lifestyle than that of a shepherd tending to his flock, idling the day away while the sheep graze. Modern-day sheep farming is far removed from the idealized shepherd's lifestyle. In fact, most sheep farmers in the United States are part-time shepherds holding another full-time job.

Sheep make a wonderful addition to the farmstead and can be a valuable tool for weed control. They provide fiber and meat, both potential side sources of income to an off-farm job. In a small-scale farm enterprise, sheep fit well into a low-input farming system because they need minimal housing if lambing coincides with warm spring weather. Starting out with a small group of ewes (10 to 20) and a ram is an excellent way to enter into sheep farming. It is not advisable to purchase your breeding stock from an auction or sales barns. Ewes at these places are usually old, diseased, or crippled and will bring heartache to the farm family.

It is best to purchase registered sheep so you can have some guarantee that the ewe or ram you are getting has been born when the breeder states it was born and so you will know who its mother and father is. Registered sheep can be purchased at their association's state, regional, or national herd shows. Another option is to purchase sheep from a commercial sheep grower who raises replacement ewes for their own flocks to replace old or culled ewes. Sometimes they raise more than they can use and offer them for sale. These growers can be found by contacting your county extension agent, a local veterinarian, or through local farm newspapers.

Breeds

According to the American Sheep Industry Association, there are more than 47 different sheep breeds in the United States. Worldwide there are hundreds of sheep breeds, each specially adapted to their own particular geographical area. In the United States, the breeds are divided into six categories according to purpose:

meat, fine wool, long wool, dual purpose, hair, and minor breeds. For the most part, the breeds are primarily divided according to meat type or wool type sheep.

Meat breeds

Cheviot: The Cheviot is a small-framed sheep with a white face and bare face and legs. It is hornless and has long wool. A mature ram weighs 160–200 pounds. A mature ewe weighs 120–160 pounds. Ewes will average 5–10 pounds of fleece.

Dorset sheep

Dorset: The Dorset can either be horned or polled. They have a medium-sized frame with white faces. Mature rams weigh 225–275 pounds while a mature ewe weighs 150–200 pounds. The fleece from a Dorset ewe weighs between 5 and 9 pounds.

Hampshire: The Hampshire breed is a black-faced, black-legged, large-framed sheep. They are widely used in the United States in crossbreeding programs when larger offspring is desired. A mature ram weighs more than 275 pounds, while the mature ewe can weigh more than 200 pounds. A fleece from a mature ewe will average 6–10 pounds.

Southdown: This small-framed breed has a light brown face and mature early into muscular carcasses. A mature Southdown ram weighs around 200 pounds, while a mature ewe is much smaller, averaging 150 pounds. The ewe will also have a fleece between 5 and 8 pounds.

Suffolk: This is the largest framed sheep breed in the United States. It has a rapid growth rate, which makes it an excellent meat breed sheep. The Suffolk has a black bare face and legs. A mature ram will weigh 250–350 pounds while the mature ewe will weigh 180–250 pounds. The ewe's fleece will weigh between 5 and 8 pounds.

Fine-wool breeds

Merino: The Merino breed is known for its fine wool, which makes great wool for clothing. Some strains of the breed can produce more than 30 pounds of fleece a year. Mature rams weigh 175–135 pounds. Mature ewes weigh 125–180 pounds.

Rambouillet: This is a white-faced, white-fleeced sheep known for its fine wool. It is descended from the Merino sheep raised in Spain. Mature rams weigh 250–300 pounds. Mature ewes weigh 150–200 pounds. Ewe fleeces can weigh up to 18 pounds.

Long-wool breeds

Lincoln: The Lincoln sheep is the world's largest breed of sheep, with mature rams weighing 250–350 pounds, while mature ewes weigh 200–250 pounds. Their fleece when fully grown spirals down in heavy locks and is coarse. The ewe's fleece weighs 12–20 pounds.

Romney: While classified with the long-wool sheep, the Romney is a good meat sheep as well. Mature rams weigh 225–275 pounds, and mature ewes weigh 150–200 pounds. A fleece from a mature ewe will weigh 8–12 pounds.

Dual-purpose breeds

Columbia: The U.S. Department of Agriculture developed the Columbia breed through crossing Rambouillet ewes with long-wool breed rams. Mature Columbia rams weigh 225–300 pounds, while mature ewes weigh 150–225 pounds. The fleece from a Columbia ewe weighs 10–16 pounds.

Corriedale: This white-faced sheep has a large frame with an ample wool coat. A mature ewe's fleece weighs 10–17 pounds. A mature Corriedale ram weighs 175–275 pounds, while a mature ewe weighs 130–180 pounds.

Other sheep breeds

The minor sheep breeds and the haired sheep breeds are not too common in the United States. The Finn sheep is an example of a minor breed of sheep. It is native to Finland and is a smaller sheep. A mature ram weighs fewer than 200 pounds, and a mature female weighs around 140 pounds. Ewes of this breed have been known to have up to four lambs at one time.

The Katahadin is an example of a haired sheep breed. While all sheep have both hair and wool, wool is the predominant fiber in most sheep. But, as the name suggests, the haired sheep has more hair than wool. The Katahadin was developed in the United States during the 1950s. Because they do not have a fleece, they are not sheared. Instead, they are used primarily for meat. Mature rams weigh between 180 to 250 pounds, and mature ewes weigh between 120 to 160 pounds.

Husbandry

Sheep are housed similarly to goats; however, goats and sheep should not be kept together in a confinement situation, as the goat will most likely bully the more docile sheep. Sheep will do well on pasture but should be provided a shelter in inclement weather. Pregnant sheep should be closely monitored, and when nearing the end of their pregnancy, they should be placed into well-bedded (straw) lambing pens to lamb.

Pasture requirements are also similar to goats, and sheep will get a large portion of their nutrition from pasture and hay. Ewes in late pregnancy or that are lactating and rapidly growing lambs will need to be supplemented with grain. Sheep do not require soda like goats, but they will need salt and minerals. The mineral copper is toxic to sheep, so read the label on your salt/mineral supplement carefully to make sure it is non-toxic to sheep.

Reproduction

A female lamb will reach puberty when she is between 5 and 12 months old. This is when an ewe lamb will first come into estrus — when she will stand for mating. Weight, breed, genetics, and her nutritional status influence this cycle. Single-born lambs, larger lambs, heavy-fed lambs, and lambs born early in the lambing season tend to come into estrus sooner because of reaching puberty sooner than twin-born lambs; lambs not fed for fast growth; or younger lambs.

Before you breed your ewes, they should be in the best health condition possible. A sick ewe will have difficulty carrying a pregnancy to term, may give birth to sickly lambs, or may not be able to properly care for her lambs. Vaccinations should be finished prior to breeding to ensure the mother can fight diseases and pass on some of her immunity to her lambs. The herd should be treated with a dewormer and have their hooves trimmed as a matter of routine maintenance. Intestinal worms are highly contagious, so all sheep in the herd should be treated at the same time to lessen the chance of having an infected sheep in the herd. Any sheep with abscesses, poor body condition, poor teeth, or any chronic health condition should be aggressively treated or culled.

The sheep's estrous cycle averages around 16 days. Standing estrous — when the sheep will show interest in the ram and stand to be mounted by the ram — is influenced by the presence of the ram and lasts for around 30 hours. Most sheep show estrous when the days are shortest. The daylight enters the eye and stimulates the brain, which in turn regulates the release of hormones that stimulate estrous. In the Northern Hemisphere, the most natural time to breed sheep is October through November. This seasonal estrous (polyestrous) is normal for most sheep, although some sheep breeds will breed all year. A ewe in estrous will be hard to detect unless a ram is present. Then she will show the ram attention (such as nuzzling him), standing still for him to mount her. One ram can service 30 females.

Lambing

The average length of gestation is 148 days. Around 10 days prior to lambing (giving birth), the ewe's udder and vulva will swell. The teats become firm and fill with colostrum, which is the vital first milk the lamb needs to develop its immune system. A ewe close to lambing should be moved to a lambing pen or "jug." This is typically a 5- by 5-foot pen that is isolated from the rest of the flock. It should be kept scrupulously clean and deeply bedded with clean, dry straw.

As lambing approaches, a thick, white mucus will discharge from the vulva. Uterine contractions will cause the ewe to become uneasy and swish her tail. She may bleat and get up and down. The ewe may start to strain as the cervix continues to dilate in preparation for the lamb to pass through. The placenta (commonly called the water bag) will finally appear at the vulva and burst, releasing fluids to help lubricate the birth canal. The ewe will strain in earnest to expel the lamb, which will come out front–feet first with the head not far behind. The entire delivery process, from rupture of the water bag until the lamb is on the ground, takes about one hour for a single birth and two to three hours if twins or triplets are delivered. The placenta should be passed out of the birth canal around two to three hours after lambing. There should be one for each lamb delivered.

The ewe will do her motherly tasks after the lamb is born. She will dry the lamb, and after the lamb stands, she will nudge the baby to her teats to nurse. Lambs need colostrum in order to build their immune system. It is vital that lambs receive this milk, which is rich in antibodies and immunoglobulins (both components of the immune system), in the first six hours after birth. The lamb's intestinal system is so designed as to allow these substances to pass from the colostrum directly into the blood stream. After 24 hours, the intestinal wall changes, stopping this process. Each lamb should receive a minimum of 4 ounces of colostrum as soon as possible after birth. Some ewes are unable to let down their milk at first. You may need to gently massage the udder for a minute and milk a stream of colostrum from the teats. Check each lamb and ewe every six hours after birth to make certain the lamb is nursing and that the ewe has not rejected her lamb(s). You should record the weight of each lamb at birth. This way, you can tell if a lamb is not gaining weight or nursing. Keep the lamb and ewe in the jug for three days to ensure a strong maternal bond and that the lamb is nursing well before releasing it to be with the rest of the flock.

Orphan lambs

An ewe may reject a lamb, particularly if she gives birth to twins or triplets, or if she becomes ill. Some ewes reject lambs for no known reason. In this case, you will have to be its mother. Make sure the orphan receives its colostrum. You will have to teach the lamb to drink from a bottle. Prepare a bottle using any of the commercial milk replacers available. If it is the lamb's first feeding, use warmed colostrum. Place the nipple in the lamb's mouth, and use your hand to move the jaws together. The lamb should soon get the idea that milk comes from the nipple and start to suckle.

If the lamb is weak or has a poor suckle reflex, it will need to be tube-fed. If you have never attempted this, ask an experienced person or a veterinarian to show you how to tube-feed the lamb, or you may risk placing the tube into the respiratory tract and un-intentionally killing the lamb. Do not over-feed lambs. They can contract scours (diarrhea) or even die from too much milk in one feeding. Lambs need about 500 milliliters of milk a day, spread over four or five feedings for the first week. After the first week, follow the directions on the milk replacer bag to determine how frequently and how much milk replacer should be fed. In cold weather, a little extra warm milk will compensate for the extra energy needed by the lamb to keep warm.

Orphaned lambs should be kept in a warm, dry, and deeply bed-ded pen, preferably within eye- and earshot of the rest of the flock. The pen should be constructed so the lambs will stay in it and the rest of the flock will keep out. This way, the orphans will not be bullied by larger lambs or even by the ewes. After they are weaned, they can rejoin the rest of the flock.

Health

Lamb care

Lambs should have their tails docked to prevent fly strike, a condition where flies deposit eggs in the skin of the lamb, which will hatch into maggots. Docking consists of using a stout, rubber ring (elastrator) to remove the tail. It should be done when the lamb is 7 weeks old. The ring is applied about 1.5 inches from the base of the tail. Male lambs not intended for breeding should be castrated by using the same type of rubber rings used in tail docking. The ring is applied just above the testicles; make sure both testicles are in the scrotum. Ask for a demonstration from an experienced shepherd or veterinarian before you perform this task for the first time.

Lambs should have access to fresh water and hay or pasture starting at 1 week old. Weaning can be started at 6 weeks for orphan lambs. Provide plenty of fresh water and good quality pasture to the lambs being weaned. At the time the lamb is weaned, it should also be given a dewormer. Dewormers kill worms and parasites, which compete with the lamb for vital nutrients and can lead to poor lamb growth. Lambs should be vaccinated against tetanus and pulpy kidney. If the mother had been vaccinated against these diseases and if adequate colostrum was fed, these vaccines can be given at 3 months of age. If not, the lamb should be vaccinated when the tail is docked. Three to four weeks after the first vaccine, the lamb will need a second injection of the same vaccine.

If you find a weak lamb, the most important steps to take are to dry the lamb thoroughly using warm towels to bring its body temperature up. Most shepherds will bring the lamb into the house and place it in a cardboard or large plastic tub lined with disposable bedding. Fill hot water bottles or a used, plastic soda bottle with hot water and wrap it in towels. Place the wrapped bottle up against the lamb. A heat lamp can also be used to provide warmth. When the lamb warms up, it will start to bleat and want to be fed.

The lamb should be fed colostrum, preferably from its mother. Cow colostrum can also be fed if the mother does not have sufficient colostrum. Return the lamb to its mother as soon as possible. An orphan lamb should be placed in a warm, dry pen with a supplemental heat source. Many people will let the orphan bunk in a box in the house or a warm basement until it is a week old. Then it will be put into its own pen in the lambing barn.

Ewe health

Viruses and bacteria causing abortions in ewes can be a big problem, and these bacteria and viruses are considered zoonotic, as they can also cause symptoms in humans. Pregnant women should never handle dead lambs or fetuses, placentas, or placental fluids. Abortions can be reduced by strict sanitation of the lambing areas and by keeping other animals out of the lambing pens. Any ewe that has aborted a lamb should be isolated from the flock to help decrease the transmission of the disease organism. The aborted fetus and placenta should be placed in a plastic garbage bag, tied shut, and brought to a veterinary clinic to be examined. Usually the tissues will need to be sent to a university diagnostic lab to determine the cause of the abortion. Some common causes of abortion include:

- **Chlamydia** causes enzootic abortions of ewes (EAE). Abortions occur during the final month of pregnancy along with stillbirths and weak lambs. Infected sheep spread it to others through uterine discharges, placentas, or fetal tissues. If there is an epidemic, the entire flock can be treated with tetracycline.

- **Q fever** is caused by the bacteria *Coxiella burnetii*. Many sheep may not show any signs of having the Q fever organism. It can cause late-term abortions along with infertility problems. If your sheep is diagnosed with Q fever, it will need to be reported to federal authorities, as it is an organism that can be used in bioterrorism. Treatment is through use of tetracycline.

- **Vibriosis** is the disease caused by *Campylobacter* and causes late-term abortions, stillbirths, and weak lambs. Treatment of an abortion outbreak is done with tetracycline. There is a vaccination available that will prevent the disease in sheep flocks. The first year, the ewes are vaccinated twice in early gestation, then once again halfway through the gestation period. After this initial series, the ewes are vaccinated once yearly after the breeding season.

- **Toxoplasmosis** causes abortions during the last month of pregnancy, stillbirths, and weak lambs. The organism is spread by cats defecating in feed or by contamination of water or the environment by cat feces. Cats should be kept away from sheep feed sources and away from pregnant ewes.

In addition to the diseases that are responsible for causing abortions, there are two diseases that can threaten the health and life of an ewe:

Pregnancy toxemia: Pregnancy toxemia occurs late in the pregnancy. It is more common in ewes that are overly fat or thin, or in older ewes carrying multiple fetuses. The cause is a metabolic disorder where the ewe does not take in adequate nutrition during late pregnancy when the lamb(s) are growing rapidly. An ewe with pregnancy toxemia will appear bright and alert but will be unable to stand. Treatment consists of giving the ewe glucose orally and via the vein. Giving ½ to 1 pound of grain to ewes in the late stages of pregnancy can prevent toxemia. Keeping your ewes in good body condition (not too fat or thin) will also help prevent this disease.

Mastitis: Ewes can suffer from mastitis, which is an infection of the mammary glands. Similar as in dairy cattle, bacteria can cause acute or chronic forms of mastitis. In acute mastitis, the mammary glands will be swollen, warm, and red. The ewe may act painful and might not let her lambs nurse. Acute mastitis is treated much like cattle mastitis with antibiotics, frequent milking, and the use of anti-inflammatory medicines. Chronic mastitis is also treated with antibiotics.

Other diseases affecting sheep

There is a saying in the veterinary field: "Sick sheep seldom survive," which sadly holds true in far too many cases. Sheep are notorious at hiding sickness, most likely because they are prey animals and often must hide illness from predators as not to appear weak. A sick sheep will give few, if any, signs at being sick until it is obvious she is ill. By then, she may be unable to stand. Shearing time is also when a thin and sickly ewe may be detected, as the thick wool hides the signs of a thin or malnourished sheep. Some of these illnesses are chronic wasting types of disease, which can become a flock-wide problem. These diseases can affect goats as well.

Border disease: Border disease is a virus that causes disease in lamb fetuses. Other names of this disease are hairy shaker disease or fuzzy lamb syndrome. It causes abortions, mummification, or weak lambs. Lambs with border disease that survive birth are persistently infected and spread the virus via secretions. The disease is first suspected when the flock begins to lamb: Fewer lambs than expected are born; the lambs that are born are small and hairy; and some lambs have tremors. There is no treatment or vaccination available. Sick lambs should not be used for breeding, but it is helpful to expose un-bred ewes to these lambs so they can develop immunity. The ewe will be able to kick the virus out of her system and will pass her immunity on to her offspring.

Ovine progressive pleuropneumonia (OPP): Ovine progressive pleuropneumonia (OPP) is a chronic, debilitating disease in sheep. Other disease conditions associated with this virus are polyarthritis, neurological problems, and mastitis. The primary route of transmission is via lambs ingesting colostrum infected with the virus. A less efficient way the virus is spread is through ingestion of contaminated food or water, or by inhalation of aerosolized virus. Clinical signs are seen in sheep more than 2 years old. The signs of OPP include chronic pneumonia, rapid or difficulty breathing, lack of a fever, and a loss of body condition despite good appetite. Pregnant ewes may have lambs that are weak or small if infected with OPP. There is no treatment for OPP, and there is no vaccine to prevent it from occurring. Control is based upon testing flocks, culling affected animals, removing lambs from affected ewes before colostrum is consumed, or else feeding lambs pasteurized colostrum and milk from affected ewes. Pasteurization inactivates the virus that causes OPP, so it will not cause infection in lambs consuming this type of colostrum.

Bluetongue: Bluetongue is indistinguishable from foot and mouth disease and is therefore a reportable disease. Foot and mouth disease is a serious illness in sheep and cattle. It is important to differentiate bluetongue from foot-and-mouth disease, as currently foot and mouth disease is not present in the United States. If it is discovered in the United States, all exports of livestock from the country will cease, and all affected animals will be slaughtered. All sheep exhibiting the signs of bluetongue/foot-and-mouth disease need to be reported. Testing will be performed on the sheep to determine which disease is affecting the sheep.

Biting insects transmit the bluetongue virus from sheep to sheep. There are two clinical diseases of sheep: reproductive disorders and a vasculitis disease of several different organ systems. The vasculitis disease causes such signs as fever, facial edema, salivation, nasal discharge, oral ulcers, reddened nose or mouth, pneumonia, lameness and stiffness, and death. Reproductive disease can manifest as dummy lamb births, abortions, or stillbirths. Prevention revolves around control the vectors (insects) of the disease. Using insecticides around the barn, promptly removing and properly disposing manure, draining stagnant water, and using insecticides on sheep will help to reduce the number of biting insects.

Pizzle rot: Pizzle rot, or balanoposthitis, is a fairly common condition in wethers (castrated male sheep) and less so in rams. High protein levels, especially when caused by feeding on rich pastures, produce a urine rich in urea, a waste product the body produces from protein metabolism. The alkalinity of the urine makes an ideal growth medium for bacteria, such as *Corynebacterium renale*, which is the primary culprit in pizzle rot, although other bacteria can cause the condition as well. The bacteria interact with the urea in the urine to produce ammonia. Strong ammonia can scald the prepuce and surrounding area leading to necrosis of the tissue. Scarring and stricture formation can block the urine flow and lead to retention of urine. Keeping the belly and prepuce closely shorn will help urine dry quickly. If the condition is caught early, removal from rich feed sources is successful at resolving the condition. Later stage treatment is rarely successful, as there will be extensive damage to the urinary tract that will be impossible to correct or reverse.

Orf: A virus causes contagious ecthyma (called orf). The most common sign is shallow ulcers, which appear in the lip, nostril, and feet areas. Lambs are most commonly infected and may be reluctant to nurse due to mouth and nose lesions. Lambs may spread the disease to unvaccinated or unexposed older animals.

In the male, lesions also appear on the penis and prepuce, while in the female lesions will appear on the vulva and teats. It is a zoonotic disease and therefore can be transmitted to humans. Orf is spread by direct contact, including breeding. Animals may be reluctant to mate due to the pain of the lesions. The disease typically runs its course in three to four weeks. Secondary bacterial infections can happen and lead to more debilitating conditions, such as damage to the reproductive tract or deep tissue infections.

Scrapie: Scrapie is a degenerative disease of the sheep's nervous system. The disease has a long incubation period before signs are noticed. It is similar to other diseases that affect the nervous system such as bovine spongiform encephalopathy (BSE) of cattle, chronic wasting disease of deer and elk, and Creutzfeldt-Jakob disease of humans. Scrapie is caused by a tiny piece of protein (prion) that is very resistant to heat or disinfectants. It is spread from infected sheep to other infected sheep, most commonly from an infected mother to her lambs. Lambs during their first few months of life are most susceptible to contracting scrapie. It is believed that some sheep are more genetically susceptible to scrapie. The disease is found worldwide and was first diagnosed in the United States in 1947 in Michigan.

Prion enters the body through the mouth. For the first two years, it remains in the body in low levels in the lymph nodes. Then it spreads to the nervous system and multiplies rapidly, causing damage to the nerve cells. Sheep will show signs such as tremors, lack of coordination, behavioral changes, and a manner of walking that looks like a bunny hop. Some sheep may be intensely itchy, rubbing against objects until their wool is worn off (hence the name scrapie). The affected sheep will die one to six months after signs occur. Sheep do not develop immunity to scrapie, so there is not a vaccine or cure. There is also no simple diagnostic test that can be performed on live animals and there is no treatment. If the disease is found in a flock, all infected ewes, rams, and their offspring are killed by the authorities; the premises will need to be rigorously cleaned; and the federal government will monitor the flock to track the progression of the disease.

CASE STUDY:
NOT A SINGLE BLACK SHEEP

CLASSIFIED CASE STUDIES
directly from the experts

Ingrid Bey and Dave Plunkett
Belle Acres
belleacres@earthlink.net
10960 W. 260th St.
Belle Plaine, Minnesota

Dave Plunkett and Ingrid Bey raise between 14 to 22 ewes on their 10 acres near Belle Plaine, Minnesota. Bey, a veterinarian, joked that they needed lawn mowers for their pastures, and sheep fit the bill. They also enjoy the fact that sheep are fairly docile animals and are relatively easy to handle. A friend of theirs raised sheep, so they were able to ask questions and observe how much work is involved in raising sheep. They started sheep farming by purchasing three ewes, each of which had twin lambs. Four of the lambs were female, so they kept those four and grew their flock. They rented a ram for the first few years before they purchased a ram of their own.

They highly recommend finding a good sheep producer to act as a mentor before deciding to raise sheep. Sheep are living animals that require care and cannot be treated like machines. Starting with a small flock and learning how to care for and keep sheep are a few recommendations prior to getting a large number of sheep. They have found that limiting factors to raising sheep include labor at lambing time, feed costs, and a lack of market opportunities.

They have found the most and the least enjoyable part of sheep farming is the lambing season. It is a very stressful time, with nightly checks of ewes ready to lamb and, despite the best of care, some lambs will die, and there will be complications with labor and delivery. But the lambs that do thrive are fun to watch as they run and jump around the pasture with reckless abandonment. They also derive extreme satisfaction that their lamb meat is delicious and wholesome. They are very proud when a customer tells them that their lamb is the best lamb they have ever eaten.

They direct-market their lamb meat to individual customers primarily found through word of mouth. They are also members of the Minnesota Lamb and Wool Producers and the Sustainable Farming Association of Minnesota. Through these organizations, they are able to list their lamb. One novel way they were able to connect with customers was through donating a lamb to an annual charity auction, which was a good source of new customers for them. Any lambs not sold to customers are then sold at the live auction barn, but they get about half the price there as they do through direct marketing.

Daily, they spend about 30–60 minutes a day caring for their lambs. During lambing season, the time commitment greatly increases. Baling hay and cleaning pen are two tasks that require sizable amounts of time. They have their sheep on a deworming schedule because parasitism is a big concern. One difficult aspect of sheep farming is that it is hard to find a shearer to shear a small flock. They ended up doing the task themselves this year and may have to continue to do so in the future.

CHAPTER 8

Pigs: The Mortgage Lifters

Terms To Know

Swine: All pigs and hogs.

Gilt: Young female pigs of any age before the second pregnancy.

Sow: Older females who have had litters.

Boar: Breeding male pig.

Barrow: Castrated male pig.

Pigs: Younger swine weighing fewer than 120 pounds.

Hogs: Swine weighing more than 120 pounds.

Piglets: Newborn swine.

Farrow: To give birth to piglets.

Sounder: Small, matriarchal groups of two to six sows and their young.

In the past, the pig was often referred to as the farm mortgage lifter. Farmers could have a ready source of cash in selling feeder pigs, market hogs, or breeding stock in a relatively short amount of time. The pig's quick growth from birth to market size is around six months, and large litter sizes (eight or more per sow) saved many farmers from missing farm payments or from going hungry. Pigs also could eat many kitchen discards, such as leftover whey from butter making, food scraps, and excess vegetables or those not suitable for table use, thus saving on feed costs.

Like most areas in agriculture, large-scale commercial farming has completely changed the face of pig rearing. The majority of pigs raised in the United States are raised in complete confinement in huge barns. Sows are typically penned in small crates so their piglets will not be crushed when she lies down. This strict confinement of sows throughout most of their reproductive life has raised animal welfare issues surrounding raising pigs in total confinement.

However, by raising pigs in confinement, diseases such as trichinosis have been virtually eradicated from the pork supply in the United States. The disease was a major public health concern for hundreds of years. Pigs become infected with trichinosis by eating rodents or soil contaminated with the roundworm *Trichinella spiralis*. Humans become infected through eating raw or undercooked pork from a pig that had trichinosis. Confinement rearing with proper manure removal and rodent control has made the U.S. pork supply free from trichinosis.

By keeping the sanitation and disease control standards of confinement rearing in mind, it is possible to successfully raise pigs on a small-scale basis. Pigs may no longer have the ability to lift the mortgage — given the high cost of land versus the low price per head of pig — but they can be a reliable source of modest income and protein for a small-scale farmer. If your goal is to provide enough pork for your family, two feeder pigs raised to market size will meet your yearly needs.

Feeder pigs, or pigs weighing around 40 pounds, can be purchased directly from breeders or through shows and auction barns. They are generally fairly cheap, from 50 to 90 cents a pound, and can be raised to butcher weight (225–250 pounds) in five or six months. Housing needs for feeder pigs are minimal. A pen with outdoor access makes an ideal spot to raise a few feeder pigs. A concrete pad — at least in the feeding and drinking areas — will make it easier to clean and sanitize when getting new pigs. Pigs will need shade in the summer and a shed or a barn in the winter.

Breeds

Pigs originated from wild boars in Asia and Europe. Wild boars look nothing like today's sleek, large pigs. Rather, wild boars have long noses, sharp, prominent backbones, and rough hair for coats. Selective breeding by humans now gives us a pig that has a higher rate of weight gain per pound of feed fed than the wild boar. Prior to the 1970s, pigs were bred to produce large amounts of lard (fat) or bacon. Now, pigs are bred to have a long carcass that is lean with a high proportion of lean muscle to fat. A pig's snout is usually long and is used for foraging and digging in soil.

They have an excellent sense of smell and have been trained to find truffles in Europe.

Pigs have canine teeth called tusks that grow quite large unless they are clipped. The eyes are generally small, and the ears can either be erect or floppy. Pigs also have a thick body and short legs. Pigs' hair, or bristles, is coarse, and they have a small tail. Commercial pig farmers will clip the canine teeth and tails of piglets to stop them from fighting and biting tails. Pigs can range in size, from an adult potbellied pig weighing around 120 pounds to huge boars weighing well over 1,000 pounds. You will want to aim for a pig that falls between these two extremes — a good weight is in the 300–400 pound range for breeding sows or around 225 pounds for a slaughter hog. Litter size can vary between and within breeds. A small litter is one in which fewer than nine piglets are born; a medium sized litter is between nine and 13 piglets; and a large litter is when more than 13 piglets are born to each sow.

There are seven breeds of pig commonly raised in the United States. The white breeds (Chester White, Yorkshire, and Landrace) are known as very good mothers and raise large litters of piglets. The other four breeds yield meaty yet lean carcasses. A medium-sized, full-grown sow weighs 300–350 pounds. A medium-sized, full-grown boar weighs 400–450 pounds.

Berkshire: This breed originated in England. They are medium-sized black hogs with white feet and white face spots. The face is dished (or slightly concave when viewed on profile), with a medium-length snout and erect ears. They produce a good-quality, meaty carcass.

Chester White: The Chester White breed was developed in Pennsylvania. These are medium sized, solid white pigs. Their ears flop forward. They usually have large litters and are good mothers. The Chester White boar is very aggressive.

Duroc: This breed is distinguished by its red color. They have long, floppy ears. The Duroc is known as a productive breed that produces large litters. They grow quickly and are very efficient at turning their feed into muscle.

Hampshire: The Hampshire breed originated in England. These pigs have a black body with a white ring encircling the body behind the front legs, forming what looks like a belt. They have erect ears and a lean, meaty carcass.

Landrace: This is a breed developed in the United States. They are white with long bodies and have very long, floppy ears. Sows have large litters and make excellent mothers. They have the highest post-weaning survival rates and the highest number of piglets weaned per mother.

Poland China: Despite its name, this breed was developed in the United States. The breed is usually black with white spots. They have short, floppy ears and produce meaty carcasses.

Yorkshire: The Yorkshire is another breed originating in England. They are usually white but can have black spots on the body. They have long bodies with short snouts and short, erect ears. Sows of this breed raise large litters and are good mothers.

Housing and Equipment

A typical pig setup includes a three-sided shed with the opening facing toward the south or east to take advantage of sun and to protect against prevailing north and west winds. A concrete pad can run from the shed to give the pigs an area to get sunlight, fresh air, and exercise. The shed should be bedded, and typically, the pigs will pick an area of the concrete to use as a toilet. However, you do not need a pen or a concrete pad to keep pigs. Properly constructed fences surrounding an area of underbrush can provide a safe, summer place for pigs. Fences can be constructed of wood, woven wire, hog panels, or electrical fence wire. Pigs love to root and will use their noses like a shovel to dig under fences. Digging down into the ground to place a string of chicken wire and installing boards along the base of the fence line can curb this practice. Remember, a small pig can wriggle through the small 3-by-3-inch gaps, and a large, 225-pound market pig can rip down fences, so your pen must be sturdy to keep the pigs at bay.

A simple, V-shaped plywood hut or even a piece of plywood nailed up against a building can provide shelter from rain and sun during the summer. During winter, in areas of the country that typically get subzero temperatures and blizzards, a sturdy shed with a good roof and solid walls will need to be provided, as pigs are susceptible to frostbite. A 12-inch-deep straw bed will allow your pigs to build nests to provide themselves with further insulation from the very cold temperatures. Monitor the bedding carefully, and remove soiled and wet bedding promptly to avoid buildup of ammonia fumes. In both summer and winter, the shelter should remain dry in wet weather. Young pigs that weigh 40 pounds should be provided with 4 to 6 square feet of shelter space. Larger pigs weighing close to 250 pounds will need 12 square feet of shelter space.

Pigs can be quite rough on equipment and like to chew or play with buckets and pans. Water can be provided in rubber pans if you only have two or three pigs. If you plan to raise more pigs, livestock fountains made of tough, molded plastic are available but will need to be installed by a plumber. These are typically square with raised sides with a shallow water trough formed on the inside.

Nipple-type waterers can be attached to a hose that is connected to a water hydrant or faucet. The hose and nipple will need to be secured to a wall or board attached to a post to prevent the pigs from destroying the hose. There are many types of feeders for pigs available. Most of these feeders can be filled with feed through a bin situated on top of a base. The feed will then feed down into openings at the base of the feeder where the pigs eat. These range from small, heavy-duty plastic feeders that hold 10 to 20 pounds of feed to large, metal feeders that hold more than 100 bushels of feed.

Feeding

A pig has a simple stomach — much like a human's. They thrive on high-energy diets with moderate levels of protein and low amounts of fiber. This is usually provided through the use of grain-blend diets called concentrates. Young pigs and those pigs being fed for slaughter are usually given all the feed they can eat at all times. They will also need fresh, clean water available at all times.

Pigs raised in confinement systems will be fed solely a concentrate diet. Those pigs under 125 pounds are given a starter ration. Those more than 125 pounds are given a growing ration. These rations can be purchased at grain elevators or through farm stores. Gilts, sows, and boars are usually fed 5 to 6 pounds of concentrate once a day. When lactating, sows and gilts may need extra feed to keep their body weight up, especially if they are feeding a large litter.

Young piglets will begin sampling their mother's food when they are a few days old. You should provide them with a space so they can have access to their own food without the mother's eating their feed. This can be accomplished through boarding off a corner of a building and allowing a 6-inch gap at the bottom for the piglets to walk under. Piglets can be weaned from their mother from 6 to 8 weeks of age, or when they reach 15 pounds. Pigs raised on pasture should also receive concentrate feed. Sows should be fed 2 pounds of concentrate a day, while gilts should be fed 3 pounds a day. When the sow or gilt is feeding piglets, they should have 2 ½ to 3 pounds of 15 percent protein concentrate per

100 pounds of body weight. Piglets can be placed on their own separate pasture after weaning at 6 weeks of age. They should be given free-choice access to concentrate while on pasture.

All pigs can be fed vegetable or fruit scraps from the garden or kitchen. However, it is illegal to feed pigs intended for sale to the general public meat or meat scraps. This rule stems from past disease outbreaks among the United States' swine herd being caused by feeding these foods to pigs. Meat and meat scraps can harbor viruses and bacteria that can cause disease in pigs.

Pigs on pasture

Pigs can be successfully raised on pasture. Grazing pigs will have natural access to vitamins and minerals found in the soil and pasture plants. Typically, these are supplemented in feed mixes purchased at feed stores, but quality does vary depending on supplier. They need less pasture per pig than typical pasture animals. Pasture raising pigs eliminates many of the negatives associated with confinement rearing such as tail biting and manure accumulation, which leads to better sanitation. The best pasture forage for pigs is alfalfa or clover mixed with grass. The legumes will add needed protein, and feed costs can be up to 20 percent less for pasture-reared pigs than those reared in strict confinement. Plan to stock the pasture at 10 pigs per acre to minimize overgrazing. Another rule is to not pasture the same land two years in a row in order to break the transmission of parasites.

During the summer grazing season, pigs will need shade. Simple shelters with just a roof will provide the pigs with just what they need. Each pig should be allotted 25 square feet of shelter. Use bedding in the shelter to let the pigs make a nest for resting. The shelters should be portable (e.g., built on skids) so you will be able to move the shelter to new grazing paddocks as you rotate your pastureland. Feeders and a source of clean, fresh water will be needed in the pasture. Water can be brought out daily or a hose can be pulled out to the pasture. The fences surrounding the pasture should be woven wire or three strands of electrified wire. Check the fences daily to prevent pigs from wandering through a break in the fence.

Reproduction

Gilts will be ready to breed when they are around 1 year of age or 225 to 250 pounds. They will come into heat at around 6 months of age, but if bred then, their litter size will be small, and the piglets will likely have a poor immune system. Female pigs will come into heat every 21 days until they are bred. Most sows can farrow two times a year. Many people like to breed gilts for the first time in the fall so they will farrow in the spring during warmer weather. Pregnancy lasts 112–115 days, with 114 days being the average. Most sows will have large litters of 8–12 piglets.

Farrowing

A pig should give birth in a clean, dry spot in a heated barn if the temperature is below 50°F. If you are not using a farrowing crate, the pen should be well-bedded with a thick layer of straw so the sow can nest. A farrowing crate is a tubular structure in which the sow is placed. She can stand up and lie down, but she cannot turn around. Both sides of the crate are lined with a space where the piglets can escape from the sow but still nurse. The farrowing crate prevents the mother from accidentally lying on her piglets, which is a leading cause of newborn piglet death.

You should check your expectant sow every few hours, starting a day or two prior to the expected birth date. After the piglets are born, their navels should be treated with 7 percent iodine to prevent entry of disease organisms into the piglet's body. This can be sprayed onto the navel, or the navel can be dipped in the solution. If you have more than one sow farrowing at the same time, you can equalize litter sizes if one pig has a larger litter than the other. Transfer the bigger piglets to the new mother, who will accept them as her own. All piglets should nurse as soon as possible after birth in order to get the necessary colostrum, which will transfer antibodies against disease from the mother to the piglets.

On the first day of life, the needle teeth should be clipped. These sharp teeth can cut the sow's teats, leading to cases of mastitis. The tails can also be docked at this time to reduce incidence of tail biting, a common problem in pigs raised in confinement. The tails are clipped using a same side pliers, leaving a tail stub of ¼-inch long. A shot of iron is necessary if the piglets are raised on concrete (dirt or soil will provide pigs with iron), as they are generally deficient in iron. An injection of 150–200 milligrams of iron dextran is given in the neck. Male piglets not intended for breeding should be castrated the first week of life.

Health

If sows are housed as a herd instead of in individual pens, pigs will live in small, matriarchal groups of two to six sows and their young. This group is called a sounder, and within the sounder two sows may pair up to feed and sleep together along with their young. Young boars will stay with the groups until the dominant boar in the group forces these young boars to leave. The young boars may form a loose group, but they tend to become more solitary as they get older. Newborn piglets also form a pecking order at the teat. As soon as they are born, they will latch onto a teat, which will remain theirs as long as they are nursing. The sow will vocalize to call the piglet to nurse; the piglets can distinguish between their mother's call and another sow on the same day they are born.

Pigs that are crowded into pens, as occurs in confinement situations, will fight and be aggressive to form a feeding pecking order. They may also cannibalize weak or injured pigs. Tail biting, or aggressively biting the tail of one pig, is also a common behavior, which leads to injury or death by infection. Allowing pigs adequate space in pens and making sure each group of penned pig is around the same size will help prevent problems. Younger pigs may also nip at their caretakers' legs. Sows and boars can also be aggressive toward humans, so be especially vigilant around sows with newborn piglets.

Diseases

Most diseases are transmitted to pigs by a contaminated environment. Feces carry a majority of the disease organisms, either from other pigs or from wild or domestic birds, rodents, and animals. A clean, dry environment that is well-ventilated will pay dividends in disease prevention. The recommended core vaccinations for pigs include leptospirosis, parvovirus, and erysipelas. For sows and gilts it is recommended they also receive an *E. coli* and atrophic rhinitis vaccination. Consult with a local veterinarian for other vaccinations recommended in your area.

Scours: Scours, or diarrhea, is a big problem with baby pigs, with *E. coli* causing most cases. A piglet with scours will have a watery, yellow-colored stool. Piglets 1 to 4 days of age, at 3 weeks of age (when immunity from the mother begins to wear off), and at weaning are most susceptible to scours. Treatment consists of orally administered antibiotics. As soon as you notice young pigs scouring, they need to be treated immediately to prevent death.

Transmissible gastroenteritis (TGE): This disease causes severe diarrhea and high death rates among young pigs. It is caused by a coronavirus, and there is no vaccination or medication available to eradicate the virus. Signs of TGE in young pigs include vomiting, diarrhea, weight loss, dehydration, and death. Older pigs affected with TGE will lose their appetites, have diarrhea, and appear unthrifty (thin with rough skin and poor growing). Treatment involves good nursing care by providing plenty of water and force-feeding.

Swine dysentery: This disease is caused by the bacteria *Brachyspira hyodysenteriae* and affects primarily young pigs. They will have bloody diarrhea, but death losses are low. Treatment is usually given through antibiotics in the feed.

Atrophic rhinitis: Two bacteria, *Pasteurella multocida* and *Bordetella bronchiseptica*, cause this disease. The bacteria live in the nose, causing inflammation and atrophy of the nasal passage tissues. This leads to signs such as sneezing, bloody noses, and in severe cases, destruction of the nasal tissue leading to nose distortion. In young pigs it can also lead to eating difficulty, loss of appetite, and pneumonia. Treatment consists of injecting affected pigs with antibiotics and using antibiotics in the feed. If a case does appear in a herd, there is a vaccination that can be given to the entire herd.

Erysipelas: Erysipelas is caused by a bacterium, *Erysipelothrix rhusiopathiae*, which frequently causes sudden death without signs. Other signs of erysipelas include a diamond-shaped rash, fever, lameness, loss of appetite, and infertility in boars and sows. Treatment is through injecting penicillin and medicating the feed with penicillin. You can prevent erysipelas with a vaccination obtained from your local veterinarian.

Leptospirosis: This disease can cause abortions in breeding sows. It is caused by a bacterium, *Leptospira*, of which there are five main types causing disease. Sows may also show such signs as loss of appetite and fever with a severe infection.

Parvovirus: This virus causes reproductive failure in gilts and sows. The embryos or fetuses may die, fetuses may become mummified, piglets might be delivered stillborn, or piglets may be born weak. It is the most common cause of infectious infertility in the pig.

Parasites

The most common internal parasites to infest swine are roundworms and whip worms. A pig with a heavy parasite infestation might appear unthrifty, rub its tail due to irritation, become thin, and have diarrhea. Younger pigs are affected more severely than older pigs due to their smaller size. A sample of stool should be taken to your veterinarian if you suspect your pigs have worms. This way, they can identify the type of worm so the most appropriate dewormer can be given to your pigs.

A good practice is to regularly deworm your pigs. Young pigs can be dewormed a week after weaning and then a week later. Sows should be dewormed one month and then two weeks prior to farrowing. If the pigs are on pasture, pastures should be rotated every year to break the life cycle of the parasites. Lungworms can also be a problem on pasture-raised pigs. The lungworm eggs are passed to the pig through eating earthworms. The worms migrate to the lungs, causing coughing, labored breathing, and a decreased appetite. Young pigs may develop pneumonia. External parasites such as lice, mite, and mange will cause skin problems. The affected pigs are treated with an insecticide. Their living quarters should also be treated to kill eggs and parasites living in cracks and crevices.

CASE STUDY: A PIG'S LIFE

Barb Eller
Eller Family Farm
12722 350th Street
Onamia, Minnesota
320-532-4946
1-800-323-1361
www.ellerfarm.com

Barb Eller came back to the farm she was raised on after working as an Army Nurse Corp. officer for 20 years. She began by raising beef and chicken for the family's use in 1997 for the flavor of free-range meat and because of her concerns with meat and poultry safety. She farms according to organic tenets although the USDA has not officially certified her as organic. In 2002, Eller began a small farm enterprise, "marketing to local folks and family members with the mission to improve the health of my local community by providing all-natural meats," she said. She direct markets all her hogs and does not use the conventional market system.

Eller started raising pigs by purchasing feeder pigs and raising them on pasture. When she started to have trouble finding local, quality feeder pigs, she did her research for the best pasture pigs and selected the Tamworth breed. She started with two gilts and raised 24 hogs. Her plans for next year are to breed four gilts and farrow two litters per gilt. She breeds her gilts using artificial insemination, and this is one of the top three time-consuming tasks on her farm.

The other time-consuming chores are farrowing and pasture rotation and renovation. Eller spends about 30 minutes a day caring for the pigs in the winter and about 15 minutes a day in the summer doing routine hog chores. The direct marketing chores take a good deal of time as well. Most of the meat is sold directly to consumers, although she is now exploring selling at local farmers' markets.

For Eller, the best aspect to raising hogs is the fact that hogs are intelligent and are very personable animals. Give a hog a good pasture and water and they can be quite self-sufficient. Her worst experience in raising pigs was getting a batch of mycotoxin-contaminated feed, which resulted in the death of one pig and a bunch of sick pigs at weaning time. Eller's organic feed supplier tests the feed for mycotoxins and delivers fresh, mold-free feed directly to her farm.

"Raising pigs would certainly be a good family project if they knew what they were doing or had a close-by mentor to help and consult," Eller said. "Certainly, the earlier the child is introduced to the pigs and they to the child, the better. Working with the pigs should probably wait until the child is steady on their feet and has learned the concepts of safety and respect. I helped feed the livestock as soon as I could walk, but always under the watchful eye of a parent or sibling. I was raising hogs by age 6 and knew which end to stay away from — and how to get up quickly when knocked down."

CHAPTER 9

Your Beef Cattle Operation

O ften, the term "cattle herd" brings to mind cowboys, the Wild West, and long cattle drives across hundreds of miles of desert and prairie. As idyllic as that image may be, it is no longer a reality in beef farming. While there still remain large cow-herds in the High Plains, there are many more herds raised on small farms across the United States. You may be contemplating a small herd for your own farm, or you may just want a steer or two to "feed up," filling your freezer with quality beef. First, you should decide what type of cattle operation you want. Do you want to start with young calves and raise them up to harvest for yourself, or do you want to sell them as fed and finished cattle? Do you want to purchase pregnant cows or cows that already have calves? Do you want to purchase a group of cows that are not pregnant, breed them, and wait for a calf crop?

Calves can be purchased as newborns all the way up to feeder calf size, which is around 600 pounds. A feeder calf is weaned from its mother and ready to be placed on feed — hay and grain — to be finished, which means putting flesh and fat on a calf until it meets slaughter weights, generally around 1,200 to 1,400 pounds. Your top priority when purchasing a newborn calf or a calf up to 2 months old is to make sure the calf has received its colostrum. Calves are born with an incomplete immune system and absolutely need to get more than 1 gallon of high-quality colostrum in their bellies within the first 24 hours of life — preferably within the first 12 hours. Scours, or diarrhea, are the main cause of death of young calves, and many cases are traced back to a poor immune system due to lack of sufficient colostrum.

No matter what age of calf you purchase, you will want to make sure the calves are in good condition, lively, and with no noticeable nasal or eye discharge. They should not have diarrhea or soiled rear ends. In addition, they should be weaned and have hearty appetites.

Calves can be purchased directly off the farm or through auction barns. It is not recommended that you purchase very young calves from an auction barn because the stress of being among all kinds of cattle along with their fragile immune system equals a strong potential for a health disaster. Dairy breed steer and bull calves are especially notorious for not receiving the colostrum they require. Older calves and cows can also be purchased directly from the breeder or through auction barns. Always ask about vaccination history, parasitical use, and calving history before purchasing. Any time you bring a new livestock purchase to your farm, quarantine it in a pen, corral, pasture, or barn for a minimum of two weeks before introducing it to the rest of the herd. This will minimize the chance of introducing new diseases into your established herd.

Breeds

Breed selection is very important in the beef industry. Branded beef, such as Hereford or Angus, is increasingly common in grocery stores in order to build customer loyalty to a particular breed. If you plan to sell your cattle commercially, buyers look for a typical beefy type of steer or heifer as opposed to narrow-bodied steer or heifer, so you may want to consider sticking to a well-known beef breed. If you want a lesser-known breed for your own use or to sell as breeding stock, you will have plenty of choices, as there are more than 100 different breeds in all shapes, sizes, and colors. Here is a small sampling of the beef breeds:

Angus: Angus cattle are solid black cattle that are naturally polled. They are one of the premier carcass breeds, yielding a high-quality carcass with nice, marbling meat. They are widely used in crossbreeding programs to improve carcasses. It is a hardy breed able to withstand harsh winter weather. The breed was developed in Scotland.

Hereford: Hereford cattle are white-faced cattle with red bodies. The white extends from the head to between the front legs. The end of the tail (switch) is also white. Most Herefords have thick, curved horns, but there is a strain that is naturally polled. They yield a good-quality carcass, and like the Angus breed, they are another premier carcass breed. The Hereford breed was developed in England.

Charolais: Charolais cattle are white- to cream-colored cattle. The breed is used in crossbreeding programs as they are heavily muscled with great carcass quality. This breed matures later than other breeds of cattle and is typically fattened to higher weights than other cattle. The Charolais breed was developed in France.

Belgian Blue: The Belgian Blue was developed in Belgium. This breed is unique in that it is one of the few double-muscled breeds (increased muscle mass compared to other cattle). Because of the double muscling, they have a high-yielding carcass, but the mothers have difficulty delivering their calves. Frequently, a cesarean section will be needed to successfully deliver a live calf. They are generally bluish white in color.

Brahman: The Brahman are distinctively different from other breeds of cattle, as they have a hump on the back and long, floppy ears. The breed comes from India and thus is very adaptable to hot weather and insects. They do not yield as much meat as the other breeds, but because of their ability to withstand heat, they are sometimes used in Southern states. The Brahman is usually red or gray-colored.

Galloway: The Galloway is typically a black animal with long, thick, wavy hair. They can also be light brown to yellow-gray. They are also a polled breed of cattle and have good-quality meat that is well-marbled with fat between the muscles. Because of their thick coat, they can withstand harsh winter weather.

Gelbvieh: The Gelbvieh has the distinction of producing more pounds of weaned calf per cow among cattle. This breed is usually one of three colors: red, black, or yellow. It was developed in Bavaria and is a fairly recent import to the United States, arriving in the country in the early 1970s. It has a good carcass yield and grows quickly in the feedlot.

Limousin: The Limousin breed is an ancient French breed. They have high carcass yields and efficiently convert feed to muscle. They are not as heavily marbled as other breeds, so they have less fat interlaced throughout the meat. They are generally red or yellow in color.

Shorthorn: As the name suggests, the Shorthorn breed was named because of their very short horns. This breed was developed in England. They are typically red, white, or roan (a mixture of red of white). They have a good carcass yield and produce good-quality meat.

Simmental: The Simmental breed are known as docile cattle. This breed was developed in Switzerland, and they have a heavily muscled back and loins. Simmental body hair ranges from yellow to gold to dark red. The head and lower legs are usually white. They have a well-yielding carcass.

Housing

In general, adult beef cattle in good condition can live outside provided they have a wind block to protect from winter wind chills. A thick stand of trees, the side of a farm building, or a solid sided fence to protect from prevailing winds will help around the farmyard. A covered shed will give them protection from chilling rain or wet, heavy snow. Pregnant cows near delivery date and young calves should be provided with a shed or a barn to escape bad weather. The barn should be ventilated to eliminate ammonia fume buildup and to provide fresh air. Bedding material, such as straw or corn stalks, should be maintained so there is always a dry layer on top. It can be allowed to build up until you are able to clean the pen more thoroughly provided there are no wet areas. Broken fence panels, bent steel posts, and rusted feeders should be removed from pens, corrals, and pastures. Cows can become impaled or entangled in these items. Fences should be maintained in good repair to prevent a curious cow from walking through a downed fence line.

Housing very young calves

If you purchase a very young calf under the age of 1 month without its mother, it should be housed in its own separate enclosure to minimize spreading disease from suckling on its pen mates until it is weaned from milk — usually at 2 months of age. These enclosures can be as simple as partitioning off a pen with cattle panels to using calf huts — plastic oval or rectangular shells — designed for the dairy calf. Regardless of what you use, make sure it is clean of dirt and manure and thoroughly disinfected. Calves being raised without a mother can be bedded with shavings, sawdust, ground corncobs, or straw. Maintain the bedding on a regular basis so the calf always stays dry. The calf will suck on any exposed surface, so make sure there are no sharp edges in the pen. As the calf moves off the bottle, and when he is eating grain and drinking independently, you can start to group the calves in small pens, or better yet, introduce them to an outside corral for fresh air and exercise.

If you use an electric fence as an outside pen, the calves will need to be trained to the fence; otherwise, they may just run right through it when they are frolicking or playing a game with the other calves. Tie bright strips of cloth or plastic to the wire between the supporting posts. This will let the calves see where the wire is located. They may investigate and get a shock, but it is doubtful they will try to cross the fence again.

Castration

Castrating male calves is a standard practice. Steers bring higher prices at market and are not as dangerous as bulls. Most buyers of male calves are large feedlot owners that place groups of hundreds of calves together. If they are not castrated, there will be many fights and displays of dominance, taking the calves' minds off eating. This focus on fighting and not eating will decrease their rate of weight gain. If the calf is already a steer, the buyer will pay a few extra cents per pounds for the convenience of not having to do the task prior to placement in a feedlot. Calves can be castrated soon after birth or allowed to grow to around 500 pounds (around 6 to 8 months of age) before castration. Castrating at heavy weights allows the calf to gain some advantage to testosterone, which in turn helps the calf to gain more weight. However, it will be harder on the calf physically to be castrated at a later stage due to the larger size of the arteries and nerves supplying the testicles.

Band castration at birth is a simple and relatively pain-free way to castrate a calf. The calf will show some discomfort when the band is placed — generally a short kick or an attempt to run away — but soon the tissue is numbed due to the constriction of the band, and the calf acts normally again. A sturdy rubber band is placed around the scrotum with the use of a special tool called an elastrator, which stretches the rubber band so the scrotum and testicles can be placed through the center of the band. The band cuts off the blood supply to the scrotum, and within two weeks the scrotum and testicles fall off, leaving a very small, fully healed scar. This can even be done in older calves but may cause discomfort for a day or two. Older calves can be castrated by use of an emasulatome, an instrument with blunt crushing jaws to sever the testicular cord without damaging the scrotum. The calf is caught, and the scrotum is exposed either by placing the calf on its back or by lifting the tail and separating the legs. The testicles are grasped and pulled taut. The emasulatome is then applied to the spermatic cord of one testicle, and the cord is crushed. The same is done to the other testicle.

The other means of castration is by open castration. This is an actual surgical procedure, usually performed without the use of anesthetic. The calf is restrained in a head gate. Someone lifts the tail, and the person performing the castration stands behind the calf. The bottom third of the scrotum is cut off with a scalpel blade. A testicle is grabbed, pulled to break the attachment securing it to the inside of the scrotum, and the spermatic cord is crushed with an emasulatome. The cord is then cut below the crushed area, and the testicle is discarded. The same is done to the opposite testicle. Open castration is a surgical procedure and does cause the calf considerable pain, particularly when it is done on older calves with larger testicles. You should have at least one helper assist you with an open castration. Calves are particularly temperamental during an open castration, and calves castrated in this manner will drop back on feed consumption for a week or two. The calf can be given an injection of penicillin the time of open castration to prevent infection. A vaccination to prevent diseases caused by clostridium bacteria is also given. The calf is then released and closely observed for excessive bleeding for a few hours. Flies or insects can also bother recently open-castrated calves, so open castrations should be timed to coincide with the end of the fly season.

Dehorning

If you have purchased a breed of cattle with horns, chances are the adults will be dehorned. Horns on a cow can be dangerous to humans if working in close quarters with cattle. Horned cattle are also docked in price at the sales barn due to the strong potential for horned cattle to cause bruising or injury to other cattle. It is easier on you and your calf if you dehorn them soon after birth. The horn will grow from the horn buds, which are two small bumps located one both sides of the forehead. Methods of dehorning include:

- **Scoop dehorning,** which consists of using of an instrument called a spoon or tube to gouge out the horn buds.

- A **paste application** consists of a caustic paste (purchased at farm supply stores), which is applied to the horn buds after trimming off the hair around the bud. A thin layer of Vaseline® petroleum jelly should be applied to the skin surrounding the horn to prevent it from burning. The caustic paste is applied to the horn buds, which will then kill the horn-producing tissue. This does sting, and the calf may try to rub the paste off, so it is important that the calf be isolated away from other calves so it does not rub the paste onto them.

- An **electric dehorner** offers a simple and quick way to dehorn a young calf. The instrument is heated via an electrical coil. The end will either have an exposed coil or a heated concave cup, which is firmly applied to the horn bud. A ring of char will form from the burn on the germinal growth area, killing the horn tissue. This will scab over, and the horn tissue will fall off in a few weeks.

These methods are effective up until the calf is 2 weeks old. Calves older than 2 weeks will need to be dehorned with the use of a Barnes dehorner. These instruments use sharp, hinged blades to slice off the horn at its base. Depending on the size of the calf and its horns, there may be bleeding. Bleeding becomes more extensive as the calf matures. Arteries may need to be pulled to stop the bleeding. If you have not dehorned a calf before, it is best to observe the process first before attempting to do it yourself. A veterinarian should dehorn larger calves and cows so the bleeding can be properly controlled.

Weaning

Weaning is a stressful time both for mother cow, baby, and you — if your home is near the cows. Moms will bawl for their babies to nurse, while babies will cry for their mothers. Calves should be weaned a few weeks before you plan to sell them. Calves to be weaned should be separated from the mothers and placed in a secure pen or pasture with plenty of water and the same grain, hay, or pasture that they ate while with their mothers. For up to a week, there will be plenty of bawling. Moms will bawl for their babies to nurse, while babies will cry for their mothers. Fence line weaning, or placing the calves and cows in adjoining pastures, may help ease the transition. The fence line will have to be very secure to prevent any cow from breaking out. Use of a solid fence, such as sturdy corral panels or wire panels and topped with an electrified wire, will help minimize fence jumping. Another point to consider when weaning is if you have nearby neighbors, you might want to warn them you will be weaning your calves. The noise can continue nonstop, day and night, and your neighbors might complain.

Handling

Being the largest farm livestock, cattle present an inherent danger. Cows and calves can be tamed, but even a tame cow can knock you over or stomp on your toes if you enter the pen with a feed bucket. Always remain on your guard around bulls. *Never* try to tame a bull or make a pet of one; they will lose their natural fear of people and can attack when you least expect it. Full-grown bulls can weigh more than a ton and are unpredictable animals. Every year, farmers are injured or even killed by bulls when they least expect it; even a tame, domesticated bull is always untrustworthy. Mother cows can also be very aggressive when it comes to protecting their babies. All duties involving a newborn calf should be overseen with extreme caution. Always keep the calf between yourself and the mom. As an added safety measure, remove the calf from its mother and put it in a safe place, such as a pen or even inside a hay ring, making sure the mom can still see you and the baby. Minimize the time away from the mom, and return the calf as soon as you are done with it.

Beef cattle are strong herd animals. If you need to separate a cow from the herd, and it is unwilling to go, try separating it with another cow to keep it company. Try not to yell or strike the cow. It takes about 30 minutes for an excited animal to calm down. Move slowly and deliberately when working with cattle. Use of an electric cattle prod to force an animal to move by giving it a shock is not recommended because of potential for abuse; if you do use one, only give a brief shock, and only shock it on well-muscled parts of the body. A rattle paddle — a fiberglass pole topped with a large paddle with small balls inside — is a good way to move cattle. They will move away from the noisy paddle when it is shaken, and its large size makes it easy for the cattle to see.

An important part of moving livestock is learning an animal's flight zone. This is the animal's safety zone. You should only work on the edge of the flight zone. If a person moves into the animal's flight zone, the animal will turn away from the person in preparation to flee. If the animal turns to face the person, the person is outside the flight zone.

If you find yourself in the animal's flight zone, step backward until the animal stops moving. To move an animal forward, take a step into the flight zone. Nervous or agitated animals will have larger flight zones. A nervous cow bobs its head up and down to watch you. It may lower its head and paw the ground, or it may try to flee from you. Calm or tame cattle are comfortable around you, stand and chew their cud when you are around, and do not move when you approach. These cattle will have smaller flight zones. If your animal is very tame, it might not even have a flight zone, and it may be difficult to move the animal at all. Cattle have a blind spot immediately behind them about the width of their hips. Try to avoid standing in this spot, as it may startle cattle, causing them to kick or flee. Another important concept in cattle handling is learning the point of balance. This is generally at the shoulder. Moving behind the point of balance will cause the cow to move forward. Moving in front of the point of balance will cause the cow to back up.

To make handling easier, you can easily tame and train your herd. Frequently walk among your cattle herd when feeding. Speak to them gently and in a low voice so they become familiar with your voice. When you move cattle, call them. Old farmers like to use the phrase "come, boss," which is an ancient term to call cattle. Using a grain bucket with a little grain in the bottom can also entice cattle to come or follow. Once your cattle get used to moving with grain, just the sight of the bucket will cause them to follow you, in hopes of getting a bite of grain to eat.

Pasturing

The majority of beef cattle are placed on pasture during the summer months. Historically, pastureland has been land unsuitable for crops. Even today, given the price of grain and the expense of hay, it is cheaper to graze pasture during the grass-growing season. Many pastures can be better managed using rotational grazing techniques, which can extend the grazing season and give you more grass yield per acre of pasture. Cattle farmers primarily perform rotational grazing.

Setting up a rotational grazing plan will take some planning. To start, grab a pen and notebook, and sketch out an outline of your available pastureland. Divide the pasture into at least six 3-acre paddocks. A moderately intensive rotational grazing plan — depending on your rainfall amount — can support one cow and calf pair on 1 to 6 acres. You will have to decide on the number of acres needed for your geographical region and on the number of animal units (cow/calf pair) you plan to place in each paddock. Once you have your paddocks planned, you will need to plan your fences. A three-strand electrical fence or a woven-wire fence with a top line of electric wire will hold your cattle in the appropriate paddocks. Be sure to include gates or alleyways to allow the cattle to move from paddock to paddock.

To be successful, each paddock will need a water source. You can use natural sources such as ponds, but using a simple irrigation pipe will provide a more reliable and fresher source of water. This pipe can be purchased at general farm supply stores in 50-foot spools of black plastic pipe. It is connected together with simple plastic fittings to make a fairly inexpensive water supply. Remember to drain the pipe before freezing weather sets in so your pipe does not split due to ice expansion. Generally, paddocks can share pipes to save on expense, so try a few sketches to make sure you do not use excessive pipes. A portable stock tank should be sufficient to hold the water, and many sizes can be found at general farm stores.

The fencing should be placed the fall before you plan to rotational graze. This will give the end posts time to settle in the ground to prevent premature upheaval of the posts. The watering system can be placed the spring prior to implementing the practice. It does not need to be buried, except at gates or where cattle may trample it or cut it with their hooves.

The principle behind rotational grazing is fairly simple. Cattle should be placed on a paddock and allowed to graze until the grass is eaten down — when approximately 4 to 6 inches is left. Then, the cattle should be placed in the next paddock, allowed to eat that grass down to 4 to 6 inches, then switched again. This continues until the final paddock is grazed. Then they should be returned to the first paddock, which should be re-grown with fresh grass. By not allowing the grass to be grazed too short, the pasture will recover faster. By forcing the cattle to graze in only one paddock, they will have to eat all the vegetation, instead of picking and choosing certain grasses or legumes over others.

Feeding

The biggest cost of a beef cow — aside from the initial investment — is the yearly feed bill. A beef cow near the end of her pregnancy can cost $1,000 or more if she is a purebred cow with exceptional breeding. Beef cattle owners always walk a delicate balance between quality feed and the price of beef. Add into the price a drought year — which dries up pasture and hay land — and you can see why cattle raising is not for the faint of heart.

Digestive tract anatomy

Cattle are ruminant animals; they rechew their food before digesting. This is why cattle can eat grass or woody material and turn it into meat and milk. The cow's stomach is divided into four parts: the rumen, the reticulum, the omasum, and the abomasum. A cow's stomach can be compared to a 55-gallon drum in weight and volume. Digestion begins in the cow's mouth. A cow only has lower incisors (front teeth) and a hard pad in place of upper incisors. Cows use their tongues to grab grass, shear it off with the incisors, give a quick chew with their molars, and swallow the wad. The grass travels to the rumen via the esophagus. The real action takes place in the rumen.

The rumen is a huge vat teeming with microorganisms (fauna), which work on the grass to digest it into volatile fatty acids and other useful nutrients. To help the microbes, the cow regurgitates frequently to bring wads of food back to its mouth to chew it into smaller pieces; in other words, she chews her cud. A cow's diet cannot change quickly — such as going from strictly grass to a large amount of grain — or the sudden food change will change the chemistry of the rumen killing off the microbes. If this happens, the cow can get terribly sick with bloat, diarrhea, fungal overgrowth, or a twisted abomasum. Many cows have been killed when this has happened. From the rumen, the food travels through the reticulum to the omasum, which absorbs some of the products from the rumen, and finally to the abomasum. The abomasum is considered to be a true stomach, functioning much like the stomach of a pig. The abomasum further digests and absorbs nutrients before passing the food onto the intestinal tract.

A newborn calf does not have a functioning rumen. It takes about four months for the rumen to develop to a fully functioning rumen. When a calf drinks milk, folds of tissue make a groove from the esophagus to the abomasums, bypassing the rumen. Introducing grain and some roughage at an early age helps the calf develop the rumen.

Grain

Grain can be supplement-fed to cattle and is used to add finish (extra fat) to a steer or cow to be butchered. Introduce grain gradually to cattle that are used to eating strictly grass or hay, as a large influx of starches can change the rumen environment, leading to serious injury or death. If you want to start cattle on grain, give them only a half-pound the first day, and add in half-pound increments daily until they reach full feed. Premixed bags of formulated feeds can also be purchased. Good grain choices are corn, oats, wheat, or barley. Never feed a cow raw soybean, as it can upset their stomach. Soybeans need to be processed (heat treated) before you are able to feed them to cattle. During harsh winter weather, grain can be fed to cattle to give them more energy. Grain is rarely needed by mature beef cattle unless hay or pasture is in short supply. Rapidly growing, good-quality pasture with a mix of legumes and grass will provide cows with the energy, protein, vitamins, and minerals they need.

Hay

Hay is essentially any dried, palatable forage. Alfalfa, clover, oats, millet, grass, and timothy are common plants used to make hay. But not all hay is equal. Hay is classified according to relative feed value (RFV). RFV is calculated by the amount of energy and protein present in the hay. Forage needs to be harvested at optimal maturity — this varies depending on plant — in order to maximize the RFV. Stem hay, alfalfa in full bloom, or plants that have been seeded out all have a low RFV. Dairy cattle, cows in late-term pregnancy, heavily lactating beef cattle, pregnant heifers, and cattle in poor condition need hay of higher RFV than stock cows. Stock cows (pregnant, non-lactating cows) and well-fleshed bulls can be maintained on rather low-quality hay because they are not growing, but they may eat more of it in harsh winter weather, stretching their rumens into a "hay belly." This will not hurt them, but some cattle can get impactions in their omasum from poor-quality hay.

Other food sources

Beef cattle can be fed other types of plant forage. Cornstalks in the field or in bales make good forage for beef cattle. With permission, a neighboring farmer's cornfield can be grazed if you are able to fence it in and run your herd on the stubble. Cornstalks can also be baled and fed to cattle during the winter. The stalks have a small amount of nutritional value, but many times, cobs of corn or the leaves will still be intact, providing good nutrition.

Soybean bales are another option. Generally, stalks will still have some bean pods, which are high in protein, and the few raw soybean pods found in soybean bales will not hurt the cow. However, they are not very palatable, and your cows may refuse to eat the bales. You must be careful not to feed supplements with urea in them, as the urea can combine with the soybean pods and make your cattle very sick. Silage can be also fed. Silage can be made from almost any green, growing plant, but corn silage is the most common form. Due to its high moisture content, silage is typically only used on the farm where it is made. If you do have a close source, it makes a nutritious, highly palatable food for beef cattle. It must be fermented and stored properly or *Listeria*, a dangerous bacterium that can sicken and kill cattle, can become a problem.

Cattle will also need supplemental salt and mineral at all times in order to replace salt lost by the body, help produce milk and develop fetuses, and help with general body functions. These are generally given in a premixed ration, either as loose granules or in the form of a block. During summer pasture grazing, only salt may be needed unless the soil in your area is deficient in certain minerals — primarily selenium. In the winter, many farmers supplement lower-quality hay or corn stalks with an energy lick. These licks consist of a protein source, an energy source, and usually molasses. They can be formulated into 40-pound blocks up to 200-plus-pound tubs.

Reproduction

Beef cattle are bred when they reach around 650 to 750 pounds or around the age of 14 months. A heifer must be well-developed before breeding, or she may experience a difficult delivery. Heifers should be carefully fed during pregnancy, as they will still be growing; you do not want them to gain too much fat, as that can also lead to pregnancy problems. The cow's estrous cycle is 21 days, and the pregnancy lasts around 280 days — about nine months.

Most cows have single-calf births, which is a desired trait because it decreases chances for birthing difficulties. Twin pregnancies occur in up to 5 percent of cattle and increase as the age of the mother rises. A female calf with a male twin has a good chance of becoming a freemartin due to the effect of male hormones on the female. This happens if during the pregnancy, the male hormones negatively influence the reproductive organ development of the female calf causing them to be deformed. Freemartin heifers are generally sterile.

Generally, beef cows are bred to coincide to deliver their calves during the late winter or spring. Late winter — February or March — calving has the advantage of having a heavy calf (around 600 pounds) during the fall market period. Most people plan to market calves soon after the summer grazing season ends, so they do not have to feed the calves the more expensive grain and hay. The big disadvantage in breeding is having a calf born during poor weather such as snow or — even worse — mud. A muddy or wet calf can quickly become chilled and die, but calves with good mothers who dry them with their tongues and get them to stand and nurse can withstand snow and cold weather. Spring calving on clean pastures helps eliminate the chilling and disease problems associated with mud and snow. Timing the breeding to coincide with your particular geographic areas warmer spring weather can save you time and the heartbreak of a calf dying.

Bull reproduction

A bull is a sizable investment and factors into half of your herd's genetics. His entire purpose is to breed your cows when you want. His reproductive health is just as important, if not more so, than other cows. A yearly, pre-breeding soundness exam is an important component in making sure your bull — or a bull you plan to purchase — is up to par for the breeding season.

Your veterinarian will do a bull-soundness exam. It consists of three steps. First, a physical examination, both general and specific for reproductive organs, will be performed. The bull should be healthy and free from disease. His feet and legs should be sound, as a lame bull will have trouble mounting a cow when he attempts to breed. The sheath and penis should be free from deformity.

Second, the scrotal circumference is measured. A larger scrotum — as long as it is normal and not diseased — usually corresponds to a higher sperm count. The final step is to collect a semen sample for evaluation. Examination of sperm motility and morphology is an important component of a bull soundness exam. Motility of 30 percent is considered the minimum amount to rate a bull satisfactory. Rapid swirling of sperm is considered very good, slower swirling good, generalized oscillation considered fair, and sporadic oscillation is poor. A sperm sample should have a minimum of 70 percent normal cells. Abnormalities in the sperm are also noted. Other cells may be seen, such as red blood cells, white blood cells, epithelial cells, medusa formation, sperm precursor cells, and round cells, and may cause the bull to be marked down in the breeding potential.

Based upon these examinations and measurements, bulls are categorized into three types: satisfactory, unsatisfactory, and classification deferred. Satisfactory potential breeders have met all minimum values and are free from genetic, skeletal, or infectious defects. Unsatisfactory potential breeders fail to meet minimum values and have defects, which will impact its breeding potential. Classification deferred means the bull cannot be excluded from the satisfactory category, as it may improve given time or appropriate therapy. Later retesting will either place it in a satisfactory or unsatisfactory category.

Health

Cattle are vulnerable to many diseases. Vaccinations, good nutrition, cleanliness, and parasite control will give you good health assurance for your herd. However, you will need to know a little about various diseases that can strike a cow or calf and how to recognize a sick animal. A healthy cow will have a good appetite, clear eyes, erect ears, clean muzzle and nostrils, and a healthy hair coat. The rumen will contract regularly (about one or two contractions a minute), the temperature will be around 101.5°F, and the cow will take around 30 breaths per minute when resting. A sick cow will pull away from the herd, act listless, refuse to eat, and may spend a lot of time laying down. An unthrifty hair coat, higher than normal (more than 103°F) or lower than normal (under 100°F) temperature, limping, arched back, and droopy ears are all signs of a sick cow.

Vaccinations

This section will name common viral diseases and vaccinations recommended for all cattle. Viral diseases are difficult to treat, as antibiotics do not kill viruses. Treatment is primarily supportive by keeping feed and water available, separating sick animals from healthy animals, and using medications to reduce fevers and inflammation. Many times antibiotics are used to treat secondary bacterial infections. Vaccinations are available to prevent many viral diseases from causing problems in your herd.

A good time to schedule vaccinations is in the fall when cows can also be checked for pregnancy. This way, you can schedule the help you will need to catch the cattle and restrain them for vaccination. A strong vaccination program is well worth the time, effort, and small outlay of money. Vaccinations are the cheapest health insurance you can give your cattle. In addition, when excess calves are sold at auction, having them vaccinated will bring a dividend to you at sale time. Buyers will have more confidence that your cattle will remain healthy when brought into their feedlots or herds if they are vaccinated.

Vaccines can come in two versions. Modified live vaccines mean the disease-causing organism is still alive but modified by the vaccine manufacturer to not cause the disease in healthy animals. This type of vaccination is considered to give a superior immune response than the killed vaccine — the other version of vaccines, where the disease-causing organism is dead but still can stimulate the animal's immune system. Modified live vaccines should not be given to pregnant cattle or to calves that are still nursing a cow. Doing so might harm the fetus. Instead, if you must vaccinate them, a killed vaccine should be used.

Prior to weaning, calves should be vaccinated with a seven-way blackleg vaccine, a five-way leptospirosis vaccine, and with a

combination vaccine for IBR-BVD-PI3. Heifers should be vaccinated against brucellosis between 4 to 12 months of age. If pinkeye is a problem in your area, calves should be vaccinated against
this prior to the start of the grazing season. Blackleg is a disease
caused by spore-forming *Clostridium bacteria*. The spores can lie
dormant in the soil for years and infect a calf when it eats feed
or soil contaminated by the spores. The spores lodge in various
organs and muscles in the calf, and when an injury occurs, they
multiply. The injury does not have to be severe; even slight bruising can cause the spores to become active and multiply. Many
times there are no signs of infection, and an infected calf may just
be found dead.

Brucellosis is a contagious disease caused by the bacteria, *Bru-
cella abortus*. It can also infect humans, where it causes a condition called undulant fever characterized by fevers, fatigue, joint
pain, headaches, and psychotic behavior. Prior to the eradication
program started in the 1950s, up to 10 percent of the cattle in the
United States were infected with the disease. Calf vaccination of
heifers and pasteurization of milk has dropped the infection rate
to the point that there are no known infected cattle at this point.
It does remain a sporadic disease in the wild herds of bison and
elk in Montana and Wyoming.

Leptospirosis

There are many strains of leptospirosis, but only five types
cause the majority of illness in cattle. In adult cattle, the disease
primarily affects the cows' reproductive organs, causing

abortions, infertility, and stillbirths. Calves may get ill with fever and blood problems.

Infectious bovine rhinotracheitis (IBR), bovine viral diarrhea (BVD), bovine respiratory syncytial virus (BRSV) and parainfluenza 3 (PI3), are viral respiratory and intestinal diseases that commonly affect stressed cattle, such as calves being weaned or sold at auction.

IBR: Infectious bovine rhinotracheitis (red nose) spreads rapidly through unvaccinated herds. Cattle show signs of a respiratory illness such as nasal discharge, a red muzzle, mouth ulcers, and a high temperature (106°F or higher).

BVD: Bovine viral diarrhea (BVD) is common in all ages of cattle, but young cattle (8 to 24 months) are the most susceptible. The primary sign of BVD is diarrhea. Other signs include dehydration, mouth sores, increased breathing, and fever.

PI-3: Parainfluenza 3 causes signs of the flu in the cow. The cow will cough, have a fever, refuse feed, and have eye and nasal discharge. Most cases are mild, but some cattle can get secondary bacteria infections leading to pneumonia.

Eye diseases

Pinkeye: The bacterium, *Moraxella bovis*, causes infectious bovine keratoconjunctivitis (IBK), better known as pinkeye. It is a rapidly contagious disease in some herds and affects calves more often than adults. Hereford cattle and their crosses seem more susceptible to the disease than other cattle breeds due to their light colored faces. Factors that contribute to the development of pinkeye include exposure to sunlight, lots of flies around the face, dust, and being infected with infectious bovine rhinotracheitis (IBR), a respiratory virus. Control of pinkeye involves controlling face flies through use of pesticide-laced ear tags, insecticide dust bags, and fly-control lick blocks. Treatment is with eye patches or injections of antibiotics.

Cancer eye: Squamous cell carcinoma, or cancer eye, is the most common cancer in cattle. Cattle with white faces, such as Herefords, are more susceptible to this cancer. Sunlight, dust, and aging are all factors leading to the development of cancer eye. The cancer may first appear as a smooth, white lesion around or on the eye. As the cancer advances, there may be a growth of rough, bumpy tissue. The tissue can quickly erode and die. If caught at an early stage, your veterinarian can attempt removal, but recurrence is common.

Neurological diseases

Rabies: Cattle are susceptible to rabies, just like any warm-blooded mammal. Due to spending a lot of time on pasture and their curious nature, cattle tend to investigate any stray animal wandering onto their stomping ground. A rabid skunk will bite any cow that tries to sniff it, and many times this is how a cow becomes infected with the rabies virus. Rabies is fatal, has no treatment available, and can be transmitted to cattle caretakers by infected saliva. Rabies in cattle takes two forms: a furious form and a dumb form. Cattle with the furious form may charge people or objects, bellow frequently, and run around frantically.

The dumb form of rabies causes the affected cow to act depressed, drool, and become paralyzed.

Grass tetany: Grass tetany affects mainly lactating beef cattle on pasture that is low in magnesium. Young, greening grass pastures seem to be the main cause of grass tetany. A cow with this disorder will have many signs associated with the nervous system. These include hyper excitability, staggering, muscle tremors, eyelids that snap open and closed, and convulsions; frequently affected cows die. Grass tetany can be a herd-wide problem and needs to be treated early and promptly. Treatment involves moving the cattle off the pasture, keeping them quiet, and giving either subcutaneous or intravenous magnesium.

Diarrhea-causing diseases

Winter dysentery: Winter dysentery in cattle is a contagious diarrhea in cattle that runs through a herd in fewer than two weeks. It typically occurs during the colder time of the year. Signs include colic, cough, decreased milk production, anorexia, and watery, explosive, dark diarrhea. Treatment is usually not needed, as the disease is typically self-limiting, although owners should make sure cattle have adequate water, feed, and possibly mineral supplementation due to ongoing losses from diarrhea. There is no vaccination against this disease, as the cause of winter dysentery is not entirely certain.

Johne's disease: Johne's disease is a costly disease caused by *Mycobacterium paratuberculosis*. Most frequently, young adult cattle show clinical signs of Johne's disease, although many cattle in affected herds have subclinical disease. *M. paratuberculosis* causes a condition called granulomatous disease of the ileum, cecum, and related lymph nodes. This change in the intestine causes a malabsorption of protein (losing enteropathy) and diarrhea. The transmission of *M. paratuberculosis* is through the fecal-oral route, but it can also be transmitted intrauterine and through the milk. Signs of Johne's disease can mimic other diarrheal or weight-loss diseases. These signs can include diarrhea, muscle wasting (due to protein loss), weight loss, anorexia, dehydration, and eventually death. There is no treatment at this time for Johne's disease.

CASE STUDY: DAIRY CATTLE ON THE SIDE

Duane Spielman
Dr. Carmen Odegaard
Evansville, Minnesota

Duane Spielman and Carmen Odegaard moved to their small farm about 12 years ago after attending college in St. Paul, Minnesota. Spielman took a job at a large dairy farm that milks around 300 to 400 cows, while Odegaard works as a veterinarian at local veterinary clinics. They decided they wanted a little extra income, so Spielman purchased some Holstein bull calves from his employer. This started a long-term side business of raising dairy beef.

Spielman and Odegaard are very diligent about maintaining the health of their calves. The calves are brought to their farm when they are 1 to 2 days old. Spielman makes certain the calves get at least 1 gallon of colostrum within the first 24 hours of life — this is the most important factor in having a healthy calf. Another important factor in raising healthy calves is cleanliness of anything the calf might touch with its mouth. This includes bottles, nipples, pails, and pens.

They prefer to keep their calves in calf huts made of molded plastic. These huts are easy to move and can be bleached between calf litters. Each calf has its own hut, which cuts down on disease transmission. When the calves are weaned, they are moved into a group of eight to ten calves in a well-ventilated pen with access to the outside. Dry air, light, and dry straw are a must in the pens.

They do not recommend purchasing baby calves from a sales barn; rather, try to find a local producer and buy calves directly from the farm. They also recommend talking with a local veterinarian to find out what reputable farms sell dairy calves — plus it is good to establish a working relationship with a veterinarian clinic in case medical advice and treatment is needed.

The most time-consuming period when raising dairy calves is the first week when calves have to be trained to drink. The calves are fed 3 quarts of milk twice a day — or more, if the weather is very cold. They will place homemade calf jackets on the calves as well to help them retain body heat. Their health will be closely monitored, as scours (diarrhea) is a big killer of young calves. Any calf that appears ill gets prompt, aggressive medical treatment. The calves will be weaned by 4 to 6 weeks of age; after this, the daily time commitment decreases greatly.

They enjoy raising dairy calves as it gives them an enjoyable part-time job with a short commute — just a few steps from the house. It also gives them a family project they hope to enjoy with their young twins, and they do not have to pay a babysitter when they go to work at this job. The cattle market is a tricky beast, though. Right now, prices for Holstein beef feeder calves (400- to 500-pound cattle) are low, and this is out of the producer's control. Spielman believes they can weather the market, and it will improve as the economy improves.

CHAPTER 10

Caring for
Dairy Cattle

Terms To Know

Polled: Typically meaning when cattle are born without horns (a genetic trait) but can be used as a general term for hornless.

Cud: A normal process in ruminant animals, which is regurgitated stomach content cattle chew on to aid digestion.

The dairy cow is the stereotypical livestock mother. The modern dairy cow has been selectively bred to give large amounts of milk, so much so that there is frequently a large surplus of milk, which drives milk prices down to below the cost of production. Modern dairy farming — at least, most commercial dairy farming — is a highly capitalized business run on razor-thin margins. Dairy pricing is a complicated process, dictated not merely on supply and demand but also on federal government manipulation in terms of price supports. Becoming a small-scale dairy farmer will take hard physical work and dedication, as cows need to be milked twice daily, seven days a week, when they are in production. You will also need to be a savvy business owner to keep production costs down while making sure your cattle produce enough milk to cover your costs.

Breeds

There are five main breeds of dairy cattle, each having particular desirable traits, which you will want to carefully consider when deciding which breed to purchase.

Holstein: The Holstein is the most familiar breed. These large, black and white (or red and white) cows are virtually milk-producing factories. Also known as the Friesian, this breed was developed in the Netherlands. It was in the United States that the breed was developed into the high milk-producing cow. The world–record holder for milk production is the Holstein. Top-producing Holstein cows produce more than 65,000 pounds of milk — roughly 8,000 gallons — a year. But an average herd cow produces around 22,000 pounds of milk a year and 836 pounds of butterfat. At maturity, the average Holstein cow weighs about 1,500 pounds. At birth, a calf can weigh more than 90 pounds. Because of high yields of milk and modern management strategies, the average productive life of a Holstein cow is short — about four years.

They can live longer, but many Holsteins encounter health problems that shorten their life spans. This is due to being confined to cement-floored buildings that are damaging to the feet and legs or being fed high-concentrate diets, which leads to foot and stomach problems.

Jersey: The Jersey cow is the smallest breed of dairy cow that is commercially milked. Jerseys are generally brown, ranging from copper to dark brown with rich, chocolate eyes. While small in stature, their milk is high in butterfat. A mature Jersey will weigh around 1,000 pounds or fewer. The Jersey was developed in the British channel on the island of Jersey. They have small calves, weighing around 40 pounds when born, and have the added advantage of being known as a docile breed. Many Holstein herds will have a Jersey cow or two in them to increase the butterfat content in the milk bulk tank.

Guernsey: The Guernsey breed is another island breed. The cow was developed on the Isle of Guernsey, which is off the coast of France. They are medium-sized, fawn-and-white dairy cows, and an adult female will weigh around 1,100 pounds. The milk from a Guernsey is high in butterfat and protein. It is also a rich golden color rather than white due to the higher concentration of beta-carotene, a precursor to Vitamin A.

Brown Swiss: The Brown Swiss breed originated in the mountains of Switzerland. It is a large, brown breed that is second to Holsteins in milk production. A mature Brown Swiss cow weighs 1,500 pounds. They produce milk rich in butterfat and protein, making their milk prized for cheese production. A Brown Swiss herd will average more than 21,000 pounds of milk per year. They are easy to take care of, doing well in all weather conditions, and they have a laidback temperament.

Ayrshire: The red and white Ayrshire was developed in Scotland. On average, a mature cow will weigh around 1,200 pounds. The breed is easy kept and is not plagued by feet and udder break-down like other dairy breeds. There is also little difficulty when birthing calves, and the calves are generally fairly strong and healthy. Ayrshire cows are good for pasture grazing.

CASE STUDY: THE MAKING OF AN ORGANIC DAIRY FARM

Dr. Dennis Johnson
West Central Research
and Outreach Center
Morris, Minnesota
320-589-1711

Dennis Johnson wanted to be a dairy farmer when he was young. He attended college, and one thing led to another; eventually, he obtained his Ph.D. and became a dairy researcher. He currently is a professor of dairy production systems at the University of Minnesota. As part of his research, he has been conducting a long-term study on organic dairy farming.

Beginning farmers have a number of hurdles when they start farming. Johnson lists the three biggest hurdles to starting a dairy farm as access to affordable, appropriate property, financial funding, and mastering the skills and knowledge associated with dairy farming. These factors should be carefully and realistically scrutinized before a cow sets one hoof in a beginning dairy farmer's barn. Another big consideration in farming in general is access to affordable health care. Most farm families tackle this issue by having one spouse obtain an off-farm job with health benefits so a family will not be ruined financially due to high health care bills if someone gets sick.

At the research station where Johnson conducts his studies, part of the dairy herd is being transitioned to an organic herd. This group of cattle is in a crossbreeding program using Holstein, Montbéliarde, and Swedish Red dairy cattle genetics. The goal of this crossbreeding is to introduce ruggedness in terms of health and foraging ability into the herd. The organic herd spends more time outside on pasture and is fed less grain and supplements than the conventional Holstein herd. This helps meet the organic standard for cattle to be fed a higher forage diet than a typical dairy herd.

According to Johnson, dairy cattle can do well spending the majority of their time outside, even in inclement weather. They do need a safe, clean indoor place to be milked, but as long as they have a windbreak, a dry and clean area to lie down, and protection from sleet, they do not necessary need to be housed in a barn. Frozen teats are not an issue as long as they are thoroughly dried prior to being let outside. An important aspect to organic dairy farming is keeping records. An organic farm needs to be certified as organic — this includes pastures, cropland, feed, and supplements. No antibiotics or growth promoters can be used on the cattle.

Johnson is optimistic about the five-year outlook for dairy farming, particularly in the Midwest, as he feels this geographical area has the most appropriate natural resources for dairy farming. Areas of rapid dairy herd expansion in the western United States are limited by water issues and encroaching human population. As long as a farmer is willing to take the time and learn the necessary skills, Johnson believes organic dairy farming is a viable production system.

Housing

Dairy cattle have typically been housed in barns. They are animals that thrive on routine and usually will have a favorite spot in the barn. Most small-scale dairy farmers will use stanchions (devices that

Photo provided by Daryl Johnson

latch around the cows neck) or a tie-stall (where the cattle are chained to the stall via a neck chain) to hold the cows while milking. Grain is usually fed to the cattle while they are in their stalls and being milked. This also helps them to associate being milked with a good thing, encouraging them to come into the barn at milking time.

Some farmers choose to leave their cattle in the barn continuously, occasionally letting them out if they have stopped milking during their dry period or for just a few hours a day while the barn is being cleaned. However, it is healthier for the cow to be able to spend time exercising, and they can be maintained well in a group setting or on pasture. The main requirements for dairy cattle are to have dry teats and a clean place to lie down. The udder needs to remain clean and can be quickly contaminated with manure if a clean top layer of bedding is not provided. A dirty udder can contaminate the milk with fecal matter and bacteria. Dairy cattle allowed access to a pasture should not be able to walk into standing water or a river, as some waters carry microorganisms that can cause serious udder infections.

Handling and Feeding

Photo provided by Daryl Johnson

Dairy cattle in a herd become accustomed to a routine, and the routine should be adhered to in order to keep the cattle calm. In every herd, there is a leader cow. It is important when bringing cows into a barn or area where they are to be milked to give them enough space to follow one another and maintain visual contact with the leader cow. Cattle rely on their vision; in fact, they have almost panoramic vision. They will hesitate to enter into a dimly lit barn or if made to walk up steps unless they are allowed time to investigate these conditions. Bright lights, shiny reflections, and shadows will also alarm cattle.

Calm cattle will be able to put their energy into producing milk and will not be nervous and jumpy when being milked. Because the act of milking places human and cow in such close contact, a dairy cow that kicks or swings her rear from side to side can injure the person doing the milking. Always speak in a low, calm voice, and move slowly and deliberately around cattle. High-pitched voices or yelling will agitate cattle. If you change the barn environment, such as by installing new equipment, changing pen designs, or pouring new concrete floors, you will need to give the cattle extra time to acclimate.

In addition to the physical danger posed by an agitated cow, a nervous or scared cow will not be as easy to milk. This will decrease milk yield and may contribute to mastitis due to milk retention in the udder. The process of releasing milk into the udder is called milk letdown. It is brought about through the release of a hormone, oxytocin, at the base of the cow's brain. In most milking herds, handling the teats by gently massaging the udder for 15 seconds is practiced to stimulate the release of oxytocin. Oxytocin affects the muscle cells surrounding the udder's milk, which produces cells causing them to contract. This squeezes the milk out of the cells into the milk ducts that drain to the teat. Within less than a couple of minutes after this action, the teats will be full of milk. If a cow is fearful, it will disrupt the oxytocin release. They will also release another hormone, adrenaline, which will block the action of oxytocin for up to 30 minutes.

Dairy cattle are fed similar to beef cattle and have the same general requirements. However, because they are producing a lot of milk, they will need to have more high-energy grain (such as corn and soybean meal) to convert into milk. Most dairy cattle produce 6 to 7 gallons of milk a day, and they will eat around 100 pounds of feed (hay, grass, silage, and grain) a day. You will want to feed a dairy cow a high–RFV value hay or good-quality pasture. They should have free-choice access to hay or pasture. For every pound of milk your cow gives, you should supplement her with 1 pound of grain. They should have water available at all times. Larger dairies will have a machine to mix a total mixed ration (TMR). All feed (hay, silage, and grain) are placed in this machine, and it is ground into a product. This way the cow will consume all feeds and not be able to pick out the feed she finds most tasty. For a person with only a few cows, the cost of a TMR mixer will prove to be too costly. A used TMR mixer sells for a few thousand dollars.

Reproduction

Dairy cattle can be bred either naturally (with a bull) or through artificial insemination (AI); most cattle are bred through AI. AI is practiced in order to improve herd genetics through use of top-quality bulls kept by stud services, which is where large groups of bulls are kept and semen is collected. Another advantage to AI is that you will not have the expense of keeping a dairy bull, and you will not have the danger of a bull in your dairy herd. Performing AI takes some training and practice. Many farmers prefer to pay an AI technician to perform the actual breeding. Dairy bulls are notoriously dangerous and unpredictable. Because dairy farmers have twice-a-day contact with their herds, a dairy bull becomes overly familiar with humans. They will lose their fear of humans and may attack when least expected.

Detecting heat in a dairy cow is a skill you must learn to accurately plan AI so the cow can be inseminated when she is most likely to get pregnant. Open (non-pregnant) cows should be observed for a minimum of 30 minutes, twice daily, to help detect heat. Standing heat is the most reliable sign of heat; this means the cow will allow other cattle to mount her as she stands. There are also secondary signs of heat, which will help you detect which cow is ready to be bred. Riding, or females mounting other females, can indicate that the cow doing the riding is in heat. Rough or rubbed-off hair on the tail head (the base of the tail) can indicate other cows are riding a cow in heat. Cows in heat may group together, follow other cows, and sniff, nuzzle, or lick the rear ends of other cows. Cows that pace or are restless may also be in heat. A string of clear mucus hanging from the vulva or smeared on the hind legs or tail is another possible indicator of heat. Bloody mucus can indicate a cow was in heat two to four days prior to the appearance of the bloody mucus. If this is seen, closely watch the cow for her next heat cycle in 15 to 21 days.

Once your cow is bred, the next step is to make sure she is pregnant. Pregnancy diagnosis is an extremely important part of cattle production. It is to your economic advantage to have an accurate diagnosis early in the pregnancy or soon after breeding so non-pregnant cows can be rebred. Pregnancy diagnosis will also help you to learn an expected due date. A veterinarian will have to perform a rectal palpation of the cow's uterus and ovaries in order to determine if she is pregnant. Dairy cattle are generally palpated for pregnancy between 28 and 35 days after being bred. Other indications of a pregnancy are a failure to return to heat when a cow's next heat cycle is due.

Dry period

Two months prior to the anticipated birth due date, the dairy cow should be "dried off," a term meaning to cause her to stop producing milk. Usually, the cow's milk production will begin to fall around this time, so you will naturally stop milking her. This will allow the cow to stop using energy to produce milk and instead put the energy into the calf developing inside her.

After the last milking, most dairy farmers will infuse all four teats with an antibiotic suspension through use of dry cow mastitis tubes. These tubes have antibiotics suspended in a gel-like substance. This will help heal any mild or chronic cases of mastitis. The cow may be uncomfortable after you stop milking her for the dry period, but she will quickly stop producing milk. During the dry period, the cow can continue to come into the barn with the rest of the milking herd. Other farmers will put their dry cows into a special area of the barnyard and feed them a specialized dry cow ration, or dry cows can be placed on pasture for fresh grass and exercise.

Calving

As a cow nears her delivery date, some changes will occur. About ten days prior to calving, her udder may start to become firm and full. The vulva and tail head may "spring," or become swollen and loose, jiggling when she walks. She may isolate herself from the rest of the herd, and she may stand with her tail raised. It is a good idea to place a cow ready to give birth into a clean, dry pen that is deeply bedded with straw so the calf is born into a clean environment. If the weather is warm and your cattle are on pasture, she can also be moved to a clean pasture.

Immediately before labor — or during stage one of labor — contractions of the uterus will make the cow restless. She may kick at her sides, swish her tail, and get up and down frequently. During this time, the cow should be moved to a large, well-bedded pen or to a clean pasture. Cows will remain in stage one labor for as little as three hours. Heifers can remain in this stage for up to three days. During this stage, ligaments relax, and the cervix, vagina, and vulva are dilating to allow for the passage of the calf.

Stage two of labor begins when the water bag appears at the vulva. The cow will start to strain and push as the calf has moved into the birth canal. The cow may get up and down or stop pushing at times. Check her every 30 minutes to see if labor has progressed to stage three. Normally, stage two of labor lasts from 30 minutes in a cow and up to three hours in a heifer. If it is taking longer for the calf to appear at the vulva, your cow may be having a difficult delivery. You will want to check the cervix in this case. Occasionally, the cervix will fail to dilate. To check for this condition, you will need to use soap and water to wash the vulva with your hand and arm. Use a rubber glove or obstetrical sleeve and gently insert your hand into the vagina. If the cervix is only dilated the width two or three of your fingers, the cervix may not be dilating properly, or the uterus may be twisted. Call your veterinarian immediately if you suspect this is the case.

If the cervix is fully dilated, and you can feel the three essential structures on the calf (two front feet and a head or two rear feet and the tail) at the opening of the cervix or in the vagina, the cow might have uterine inertia or poor uterine contractions. You can use two clean pieces of soft, nylon rope to make a slipknot above the lower joint (fetlock) of the legs and a half-hitch loop below the fetlock. Apply moderate traction to assist in the delivery. Do not use excessive force or a tractor to apply traction. Time your pulls with the cow's attempts to push. If you are unsuccessful after two or three attempts, call your veterinarian.

Stage three occurs when the calf appears at the vulva. Normal delivery position of a calf is front–feet first with the head resting between the legs. Occasionally, a calf will deliver hind–feet first. This is a normal variation and should not be cause for concern as long as both back feet are coming at the same time. Dystocia occurs when the calf is presented in strange positions. Sometimes a foot will be flexed back, but it can easily be corrected by pulling the foot into the normal position. Other calves can have legs bent back, a head twisted to the side, rear end coming first, or the calf lying across the birth canal. These types of presentations will need to be corrected by a veterinarian to protect the uterus from tears and to minimize damage to the calf.

Stage four is the passing of the placenta. Many cows will consume the placenta, and it usually does not cause any problems. One of the important last points to do in a birth is to check the uterus for a second calf by slipping a clean, gloved hand into the birth canal. Many times, twins can cause the birthing difficulties a cow may be having. If the labor was difficult, the uterus and vagina should be checked for tears or excessive bleeding. If there are tears in the wall of the uterus or large amounts of blood coming out of the vagina, call your veterinarian for treatment.

Check the calf after delivery. Make sure all mucus is removed from the mouth and nostrils. The calf should be blinking and attempting to lift its head immediately after delivery. If the calf is not breathing, use a piece of straw to tickle its nose. If that fails to stimulate a breath, you can try chest compressions or even mouth-to-snout breathing. When the calf takes a breath, stop rescue breathing. If a calf is gurgling fluid, drape the lower half of the body over the side of a pen or two bales of hay or straw so the head hangs down below the upper body. This will let fluid escape from the respiratory tract. Chest compressions while the calf is draped can also help with breathing. Get the cow up or gently drag the calf to the cow's head so she can begin cleaning and drying the calf off. You should dip the calf's umbilical cord stump in a tincture of 2.5 percent iodine. The calf should consume 1 gallon of colostrum within its first 12 hours of life.

Problems associated with calving

Uterine prolapse: A uterine prolapse occurs when the cow strains and pushes her uterus out of her body. It is unmistakable when this occurs, as a large muscular sac will protrude or hang down from the vulva. When this happens, call your veterinarian immediately; it is an emergency. Pen the cow up to prevent her from injuring this fragile organ and prepare for the veterinarian's arrival by removing soiled bedding and laying down a deep layer of fresh bedding. The veterinarian will attempt to replace the uterus. The majority of uterine prolapses can be successfully replaced provided medical attention is promptly received. The cow can bleed to death if the uterine artery was torn when the prolapse occurred. Occasionally, after replacement the cow will continue to strain and push the uterus back out. The veterinarian may stitch the vulva shut and give the cow medicine to contract the uterus to prevent this from happening.

Hypocalcemia: Hypocalcemia, or milk fever, can occur soon after calving especially in older dairy cattle. The udder can make such huge demands for calcium that it depletes the calcium in the cow's blood stream to the point that she becomes weak or is unable to stand. Calcium is needed for muscle contractions. A cow with milk fever is weak, wobbly, and will have cold ears. Some cattle might be restless, and may pace and bellow. Milk fever is treated with calcium given in the vein and possibly supplemental oral calcium gel. Calcium can be purchased at local veterinarian offices or at farm supply stores.

Calving paralysis: Calving paralysis occurs when nerves in the cow's pelvis are injured during delivery. Heifers are more prone to calving paralysis due to their smaller pelvic opening. Signs can range from a weak leg to not using a leg to an inability to stand. If you suspect calving paralysis, call your veterinarian for treatment. Treatment consists of injections of steroids and non-steroidal, anti-inflammatory drugs to reduce inflammation of the affected nerves. Another important component of treatment is excellent nursing care. If large cows lie on one side for more than four hours, the muscles on the down side can die because of the extreme pressure exerted by the cow's weight. This damage can be prevented by placing a deep layer of straw bedding — greater than 12 inches should suffice — and turning the cow from side to side every four hours. Straw bales can be used to prop the cow on her side as well. The cow should have access to water and hay while down. She should be goaded to stand as well. You can assist her attempts to stand by grasping the tail at the base and lifting as she tries to rise.

Retained placenta: A cow will normally pass her placenta within six hours after the birth. If she has not expelled the tissue after 12 hours, it is considered retained. As long as the cow is healthy, eating, and does not have a fever, it is best to trim off any placenta protruding from the vulva. It should be expelled within a week after calving. If the cow with a retained placenta stops eating, ceases milk production, or runs a fever, call your veterinarian for treatment. Removal of a retained placenta is not recommended. Instead, the veterinarian may use drugs to try to get the uterus to release the retained bits of placenta. The cow will also be placed on antibiotics and anti-inflammatory drugs to combat infection.

Health

Udder anatomy

The udder of a dairy cow is an amazing thing. It is more than four teats and an udder (commonly called a bag) — it is a rich factory, producing milk, butterfat, and protein with a generous blood supply. Because it is the primary focus of the dairy cow, it is important for the dairy farmer to understand how the udder works. The udder is divided into two fore and rear quarters. Looking from behind, it is divided into two halves by the mammary groove.

A suspensory system maintains the udder in proper alignment with the body. It needs to be strong to support the udder, which may weigh as much as — or more then — 100 pounds in a mature Holstein cow. If this supporting structure breaks down, the cow is more prone to teat or udder injury, and more susceptible to mastitis.

The teats are at the ends of each quarter. They function as a valve for the release of milk and to provide for the suckling of a calf. They are smooth and hairless. The streak canal is the duct through which milk exits the gland and is the major defense against the introduction of mastitis-causing organisms. During milking, the sphincter muscle of the streak canal relaxes to allow milk release. It remains open for about an hour after milking. Using a post-milking germicidal solution on the teat will protect the streak canal from being invaded by bacteria.

The vascular system of the udder is vast. The large mammary arteries are easily seen on the side of the udders. They are susceptible to injury from overgrown feet and dewclaws, the claws located at the side of the foot above the hooves. Ducts and cisterns drain the milk from the secretory tissues, which make up the majority of the udder.

Hoof health

Photo provided by Daryl Johnson

Large commercial dairy farms have many problems with cattle hooves due to nutritional problems, a life spent on concrete, and wet conditions in the barns. With a small-scale farm, hoof health problems can be just as severe if you do not pay attention to the hoof. Cattle with sore feet will not eat as well, will be in pain, and are susceptible to develop other leg problems. A normal cow's hoof should be rounded at the tip — not overgrown on the sides — and the skin between the toes should be a healthy pink-white. An unhealthy hoof will be over-grown at the tip and sides. The skin between the toes may ooze fluid from infection, may have reddened tissues, or may have a foul odor.

If a cow is allowed to exercise, foot problems should be minimal. If a cow does become lame or its hoof overgrows, a foot-trimming session should be planned. You can attempt to trim the hoof your-self, or you can hire a professional to do the job. A large-animal veterinarian should be able to examine your cow's hoof. Another option is to hire a hoof trimmer, who has the tools to come to your farm to restrain and examine your cow's feet. Either profes-sional will check for such things as sole ulcers, injuries, warts, or infections. They can instruct you as to the best treatment strategy for your cow and will likely trim the cow's hooves.

Mastitis

Mastitis in dairy cattle causes considerable economic loss to the dairy farmer. Infection with bacteria is the main cause of mastitis. Many factors contribute to mastitis in dairy cattle, including poor milking techniques, teat injury or sores, faulty milking machines, and high exposures to bacteria. Signs of mastitis include swell-ing, heat, and pain in the udder. Severely sick cattle will lack an appetite, be weak, and may not be able to stand. The milk from the affected quarter(s) may be watery, chunky, or have flakes. Other cases of mastitis will be a subclinical, chronic form, which will not make the cow sick but will cause increased somatic cell counts in the bulk tank.

A California Mastitis Test (CMT) kit will help you determine if your cow has mastitis. This kit comes with a paddle with four shallow wells. Milk from each quarter is stripped into each well, and a solution is squirted into the milk. The paddle is swirled. Milk with mastitis will react with the solution and cause gelling. These kits can be purchased at livestock veterinarian offices, at farm supply stores, or through online farm supply companies.

Staphylococcus aureus causes a large amount of mastitis cases, both acute and chronic, in dairy herds. It is a hard bacterium to eradicate from the quarters. Streptococcus bacteria also cause mastitis and are spread from cow to cow or through dirty living environments. Coliform mastitis can cause a cow to become extremely ill through the release of toxins. The cow will become weak and may not be able to stand. It will stop eating and cease to have rumen contractions. A veterinarian should promptly treat this type of mastitis in order to save the cow's life.

Preventing and controlling mastitis

Good milking procedure, fine-tuned milking machines, and a clean environment should eliminate most cases of mastitis. All people who milk and care for the dairy cow should be trained to properly prepare the milking cow for milking and to spot signs of mastitis. Mastitis is the biggest health problem of the dairy cow because it decreases milk production and can make the milk undrinkable or unsalable.

Prior to milking, the udder should be cleaned with a soft, disposable cloth to remove any dirt and debris. If there is any dirt present on the teats, they should be carefully cleaned and lightly disinfected. Dry the teats well before milking by hand or placing the milking unit on the teat.

After milking, each teat should be dipped in a post-milking dip solution. This solution is usually an iodine-based liquid and can be readily found in any dairy supply store. Cows should be fed or allowed access to pasture or hay after milking. They should be encouraged to stand for at least an hour after milking to allow time for the teat sphincter muscle to close. This will prevent any bacteria from the ground from traveling into the teat if the cow lies down.

The barn, feedlot, or holding pens where cattle congregate should be scraped or cleaned of manure at least twice daily. Manure should not be allowed to accumulate where dairy cattle are held. Bedding should be changed frequently to keep the cattle on a clean, dry layer of bedding. Fly and insect control is another means to stop the spread of mastitis. Flies can harbor some of the organisms that cause mastitis.

If your dairy cow is allowed pasture access, do not let it have access to ponds or streams. Wading in ponds or standing in water can expose the udder and teats to water borne organisms, which can cause hard-to-treat cases of mastitis. A dairy cow's feet should be regularly trimmed. This includes the dewclaw. Sharp edges on a hoof can damage teat ends or the udder, especially in cattle with low-slung udders when they walk, lie down, or attempt to stand. Using a handheld propane torch, some farmers will singe the hair on the udder to keep dirt and manure from accumulating on the udder. If you use a milking machine, all parts of the machine should be regularly serviced and checked daily for any faults. Rubber parts showing signs of wear should be promptly replaced. The vacuum setting both on the compression unit and at the teat end should be carefully calibrated. All equipment should be washed, sterilized, and properly stored immediately after milking has ended.

Treating mastitis

Mastitis is treated with pre-packaged mastitis tubes that are widely available at veterinarian office or general farm supply stores. The tubes contain antibiotics and have a special tapered end, which inserts easily into the canal of the teat. It is imperative that the teat and the end of the teat be washed free of dirt, manure, and other foreign matter, and the end of the teat repeatedly swabbed with alcohol before inserting the tube into the teat canal. The cow will need to be restrained in a stanchion, with a halter, or in a cattle chute. If the cow is not used to humans handling her teats, it is wise to have a second person perform tail restraint on the cow while you clean the teat and insert the tube end into the teat opening. After inserting the tube, the plunger on the end of the tube is slowly pushed in, allowing the medicine to enter the teat canal.

CASE STUDY:
THE COW SENSE

Daryl Johnson
Evansville, Minnesota

Daryl Johnson got started in dairy farming at an early age. His parents were dairy farmers, and when he was ready, he took over the family farm outside Evansville, Minnesota. Johnson milks around 60 Holstein cows twice a day, 365 days a year. He has been through many financial cycles during his years of dairy farming; right now, the dairy industry is in a downward cycle, with low milk prices making dairy farming a shaky prospect.

However, Johnson feels that this downward cycle might be a good time for a beginning farmer to start up a small-scale dairy farm. Unlike just a few years ago, prices of dairy heifers and cows are reasonable, and feed prices are going down as well. Both these factors are among the biggest expenses of dairy farming. Another big expense is land, which is needed to spread cattle manure on, to make hay for the cattle, and to grow crops.

Dairy farming is a capital-intensive business. The majority of dairy farmers will need a close working relationship with their banker or financial institute to make sure they have enough money for needed equipment, grain, and cattle. In addition to cattle, land, and capital, there are other necessary items to make it as a small-scale dairy farmer. A barn with tie stalls is sufficient for a small dairy herd like Johnson's. A parlor barn with free stalls is another option but is more costly to construct. A manure-handling system will greatly reduce the labor-intensive part of manure removal from the barn. While a stave silo is almost iconic on a dairy farm, using bags or a bunker system is a cheaper way to store silage. One item that will pay off in the end is a total mixed ration (TMR) mixer — Johnson definitely recommends this piece of equipment.

He attests that the best part about dairy farming is the lifestyle and working with the cattle. Johnson spends about 14 hours a day working on his farm along with a full-timed hired hand. His top three time-consuming chores are heat detection, feeding the cattle, and putting up feed. This is in addition to the milking chores and calf-feeding duties. A dairy farmer has to be fully committed to the farm in order for it to work successfully.

Having "cow sense" is a must as well, as a healthy and comfortable cow gives more milk. In Johnson's opinion, the worst aspect about dairy farming is having a cow develop feet and leg problems and not knowing why this occurs. He uses artificial insemination (AI) to breed his cows. He tries to pick sires that will improve the feet and legs of the calves, but despite this, he still has cows that have feet and leg problems.

CHAPTER 11

Medicating
Your Livestock

As a livestock owner, eventually you will be faced with having to administer medicine to your animal. It can be scary when facing a 1,000-pound beast and being expected to pop a pill down its throat or jab it with a needle. Even if you are an organic livestock farmer, the wise owner will vaccinate their livestock against common diseases, so at some point or another you will have to take the plunge and confront the task. To save on veterinary expenses — or if you do not live near a veterinarian — you can learn the basics in delivering medications and vaccines to your livestock. Though some methods of administering medicine are fairly simple and easy to grasp, other methods are more difficult and best left to trained personnel to prevent injury to the animal.

Photo provided by Duane Spielman

Before you begin to treat your animal, it is vitally important that safety takes precedence over treatment and that you know the temperament of your animal. If you are unable to handle your animal with ease on a daily basis, it is best to let a more experienced person medicate it, even if it means traveling a long distance or bringing the veterinarian to your farm. For example, it is unwise for the average person without a strong, secure chute and plenty of experience to examine or treat bulls. They are too unpredictable and strong to safely handle. If your animal is docile and trained to a halter, or you have a chute with a securely mounted head gate, proceed with caution as you secure it with a halter to a sturdy post or catch it in the head gate.

Livestock medication comes in many forms. There are oral medications such as pills, drenches, gels, and pastes. Injections can be given in the muscle or under the skin. Some medicines such as antiparasitics (dewormers) can be poured directly onto the skin of the back to be absorbed. Some antibiotics and various types of fluids can be given directly into a vein, and medicine can be infused into the mammary glands via the teat canal.

Administrating the Medication

Once the type of medication and route of administration is decided upon, you will need to assemble the equipment needed to treat the animal. Oral treatments are administered via balling gun, mouth speculum, drench bottles, or gel or paste tubes:

- A **balling gun** is a metal or plastic tube-like device with a large end for holding pills or boluses. A plunger runs down the middle of the tube to force the pill out of the end.

- A **mouth speculum** is a hollow metal tube, similar to a vacuum cleaner tube. It is used to give cattle very large pills or capsules, or to pass stomach tubes into the esophagus.

- **Drench bottles** are plastic or glass bottles with a long neck. They are used to give animals liquids.

- **Gel or paste tubes** come in a similar shape to a caulking tube and are delivered into the mouth through the use of a caulking gun. Always have a bucket of warm water to lubricate the tools you are using.

To give oral medications to goats, sheep, or cattle, you will stand to one side of the animal. Slowly reach over the animal's head with your less dominant hand and grasp the edge of the lower jaw with your hand. Hold the head tightly to your body while you brace your feet at least a shoulders width apart. Holding the animal's head tightly will prevent it from swinging its head.

Advance the hand holding the jaw toward the mouth, and place your hand between the lips, right behind the lower incisors. There is a smooth gap between the teeth in front of the jaw and the molars in the back of the jaw. Press on the roof of the mouth, and the animal will open its mouth. Gently introduce the instrument you are using to give the medication into its mouth and direct it toward the back of the throat. When you reach resistance, stop, and administer the medicine. You can injure the animal's throat or roof of the mouth if you exert too much force in inserting the instrument.

Drench bottles or gel or paste tubes can be placed in the corner of the mouth in the gap between the teeth. Hold the head straight and parallel with the ground. The medicine then can slowly be squeezed from the bottle or tube. Allow the animal to swallow the medicine after a generous dose has been given. It may take two to three tries before the animal will swallow the entire dose. Oral medications can also be given via a stomach tube, which goes through the oral cavity, down the esophagus, and directly into the stomach. This is a much more complicated procedure and is best demonstrated before any attempt is made to treat an animal in this fashion. Have a veterinarian or more experienced livestock owner show you how to pass a stomach tube. The tube can be inadvertently passed into the trachea, or windpipe. If this happens, medicine can enter the lungs leading to lung damage, hard-to-treat pneumonia, or death.

Many medications are administered to livestock via injections. Antibiotics, vaccinations, an anti-inflammatory, reproductive medications, vitamins, and calcium are all examples of medications given via needle into the muscle or under the skin. Read the medicine labels carefully to determine the route of administration or consult your animal care provider if you have questions. For muscle or skin injections, you will need to assemble isopropyl rubbing alcohol, cotton balls, the medication, appropriate sized needles, and syringes.

Injections

On full-grown cattle, a 16-gauge needle that is 1- to 1 ½-inches long is needed for thick liquids while an 18-gauge needle of the same length is appropriate for thinner liquids. Use shorter needles for subcutaneous (under the skin) injections and longer needles for intramuscular treatments. Small calves, goats, and sheep require ⅝-inch, 18-gauge needles for subcutaneous injections. If an intramuscular injection is given, use a 1-inch, 18-gauge needle. Using too long of a needle can increase the potential that the needle will break off inside the animal if it moves while you are injecting medicine. Do not reuse needles; one-use needles are fairly inexpensive and lessen the chance for abscess formation from a contaminated needle.

Again, proper restraint and control of the animal is imperative with injections. In order to not cause scarring to prime cuts of meat, intramuscular injections should be given in the neck, about midway between the head and the front leg, and in the middle third of the neck for adult cattle. For sheep, goats, and small calves' injections, subcutaneous injections should only be given in the neck. Try to avoid intramuscular injections if at all possible due to the smaller muscle mass in these animals. These types of animals can have severe irritation and stiffness when injections are given in the muscle.

Cattle can also be injected in the caudal thigh muscles, provided you can protect yourself from being kicked. To add a little extra security, sometimes tail restraint, or tail jacking, can be used by a second person who holds the tail straight up near the base. This maneuver makes it difficult for cattle to kick. Be careful not to put too much pressure on the tail, as you can damage the nerves and muscles.

Once you have determined your injection site — an area free of manure and moisture — swab the area with isopropyl alcohol. Remove the needle from the syringe if you have attached it to the syringe and remove the cap. Hold the needle by the hub with your thumb and forefinger, and quickly jab the needle into the selected site. Check that no blood appears in the hub. If blood appears, repeat the needle stick at a different site to avoid inject-ing the medication into the blood stream, which can be deadly. Attach the syringe to the needle and inject the medication. Up to 20cc of medication can be injected into one site in adult cattle; no more than 10cc should be given in one spot for goats, sheep, and calves.

Subcutaneous injections of certain medications and some calcium solutions can be given in the loose skin on the front of the neck or in the loose skin in the chest area on the side of the animal be-hind the front legs. Safely secure the animal and prepare the site as you did with intramuscular injections. Then insert the needle into the skin almost parallel to the body until it pops through the inner side of the hide. Up to 125cc of calcium solution can be given to adult cattle under the skin in this manner. Do not give more than 50cc in any one spot for the smaller livestock For thicker medications like penicillin or tetracycline, no more than 30 to 35cc should be given in one spot for cattle; 15cc is enough of a dose for smaller cattle. *Never* inject dextrose-containing solutions (sugar solutions) under the skin. Abscesses, cellulitis, or skin sloughing can occur in these cases.

Many medications can also be given directly in the vein, but that is best learned by direct observation, due to the danger of causing bleeding from an injured vein and the possibility of injecting medicine directly into the neck artery.

There are other routes of medicating cattle that the average cattle owner can tackle. Deworming medication and lice control have been conveniently formulated in a pour-on solution which is, as the name suggests, poured along the top of the animal's back. Nothing could be easier, as long as directions listed on the medicine bottle are followed closely. Usually you will need to do this on a dry day and keep the animal dry for up to 24 hours after treatment to prevent the solution from washing off the skin.

An important item to note is drug withdrawal times. Many antibiotics will have a withholding time before your animal can be sold for meat or before the milk can be sold. Meat packing plants and milk plants regularly test for antibiotic use. If it is found that you sold an animal that still has antibiotics in its system, you may be fined. Milk processing plants may force you to pay for milk that was comingled with your milk, as the entire load will need to be discarded. At the very least, you will get a visit from your local Food and Drug Administration representative.

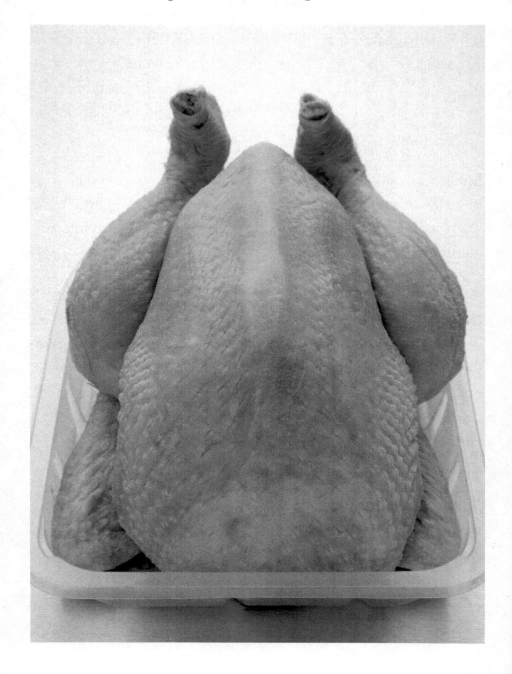

CHAPTER 12

Butchering Livestock

Harvesting Chickens

When your broilers are ready to be butchered (around 8 weeks of age), you will need to prepare your processing area. It does not have to be elaborate, but it needs to be clean, free from insects, and have a water supply. Processing is a three-step procedure consisting of the actual butchering, evisceration, and chilling. The butchering process should be done in a separate room from the last two steps.

You will need to gather supplies before starting. You will need two large containers, such as clean 5-gallon buckets or even clean metal garbage cans. One will be used for scalding and another will be used for chilling. You will also need two or more large stockpots for boiling water and a sturdy worktable. It is best if the worktable is made from an impervious material to protect it from the water and so it can be bleached before and after use. Other equipment and supplies include sharp knives, two or more deep pans, a cutting board, a permanent marking pen, and freezer bags.

Fill the stockpots with water and bring to a boil prior to butchering. Once you have selected your chickens for butchering, you will need to sever its throat. A sharp axe makes a clean cut but does not allow as much to bleed out as does a sharp knife. Regardless of the method used, you should hold the carcass upside down to allow the blood to drain out. The throat is cut with the sharp knife right below the lower jaw. There are also killing cones or shackles available to help hold the chicken steady during the butchering process. The chicken will flop around for a minute or two after butchering, so do not be alarmed.

Once the chicken is butchered, hold it by the legs and immerse it, head first, in the scalding water for 30 to 60 seconds. The carcass then should be moved around in the water to make sure the water thoroughly penetrates all the feathers. This allows the feather follicles to relax and makes feather removal easier. You may want to wear hand and arm protection to keep the water from scalding your skin. You should then suspend the scalded carcass by the legs with shackles or rope to make picking out its feathers easier. The feathers should be picked as soon as possible after scalding. The feathers can be picked or rubbed off, but whatever process is used, be careful not to tear the skin. Pinfeathers can be removed by using a dull knife and your fingers. Usually, on young broilers, the skin will be free from hairs once the feathers are picked. On older chickens and turkeys, there may be some fine hairs on the skin after the feathers are removed. These can be removed by singeing the carcass using a handheld propane torch. Move the flame quickly over the carcass to avoid burning the skin. Be careful not to burn yourself in the process.

Once the feathers have been removed, it will be time to eviscerate or remove the internal organs from the body. First, the head should be cut off. Find the joint between the head and the first neck vertebra by gently flexing the neck. Use the knife to find where the joint is (there will be a slight depression between the vertebra) and cut through the tissue. Do not try cutting through the bone, or you will dull your knife and possibly cut yourself in the process. Place the chicken belly down on your cutting board or table. Insert the tip of a knife in the skin near the point of the shoulder and slice the skin open all the way to the tip of the neck. Pull the skin loose from the neck and pull the crop, esophagus (gullet), and windpipe (trachea) loose. Cut them off where they meet the body and discard. Remove the feet next. Turn the chicken over so the belly is up, bend the foot back at the hock joint, and cut through this joint to remove the feet. The feet will have bones, so they should be thrown away in the trash. Turn the bird back over and remove the oil gland at the base of the tail. You will notice the opening of the oil gland. Start a cut 1-inch up the body from this opening and cut deep into the vertebra and make a scooping cut to remove the gland.

The abdomen will next be opening. Place the chicken belly up, pull the abdomen skin up near the tail, and cut through the skin and body wall, being careful not to penetrate into the abdominal organs. Extend the cut to the tail near the vent. Cut around the vent and meet your first cut at the top of the vent. Pull the vent and the end of the large intestine out of the abdomen, but do not break the intestine. Let go of the vent and stick your hand inside the abdominal cavity as far as possible. Break the attachments of the intestines to the abdominal wall. Grasp the heart and pull the abdominal organs out, twisting gently as you bring them out. The gizzard, heart, and liver (giblets) can be removed from the abdominal organs and saved for eating. Discard the rest of the organs. Peel the excess fat and the lining from the gizzard. Trim the heart sac and blood vessels from the heart. Carefully trim the gallbladder off the liver. Wash the giblets and place them in pan of cool water.

Next, remove the lungs from the body wall. They are located near the backbone on each side. Stroke two fingers along this area to remove, then discard. The reproductive organs are located near the backbone as well. They should be removed and discarded. Use a running hose or faucet to rinse the carcass inside and outside. Place it in the chill water container. This water should be changed frequently if you are butchering more than two or three birds. You can also place a slowly running hose in the chill water container and let it overflow as you are processing birds.

Once the birds are properly chilled they can be further cut up into parts, or they can be packaged in sturdy freezer bags. Place the giblets inside a small plastic food bag and place this inside the body cavity. Excess water should be drained from the carcass before placing inside the freezer bag. Slip the excess neck skin over the exposed neck bone to keep it from puncturing the bag. Place in freezer to preserve.

Game birds and waterfowl

Butchering turkeys, guinea fowl, and game birds is similar as for chickens. Likewise, harvesting, cleaning, and storage of chicken eggs apply to guinea fowl and game bird eggs. Game birds are often sold live to hunt clubs or hunting preserves. The birds are typically sold at around 16 weeks of age, although the hunting preserve may have different requirements. It is very important that you check prior to release with your state's Department of Fish and Game regarding the regulations governing the release of game birds in your state.

Butchering ducks and geese is very similar to butchering chickens. Pekin ducks can be ready to butcher at 8 weeks of age when they are 5 pounds. Rouen ducks mature much more slowly and will be ready for butchering at 5 to 6 months. Geese are usually raised for the holiday market during the late fall. They should be 5 to 6 months old and weigh 10 to 15 pounds, depending on the breed. The down from the breast area can be washed, dried, and saved for use in pillows or clothing. After butchering, geese and ducks can be dry picked, but scalding the feathers first makes them release easier and cuts down on skin tears. If you do not want to save the down, the goose or duck can be waxed after the large feathers are removed. This process will remove the down and smaller feathers that are more difficult to remove. Melted paraffin wax can be purchased and heated to 140–155°F. The goose or duck should be dipped twice into the wax, then dipped into cold water to set the wax. When the wax sets to a flexible form, it can then be stripped off along with the down and feather. The wax can be strained off the feathers and down and reused.

Harvesting Rabbits

If your plans include slaughtering rabbits for sale to commercial businesses, such as grocery stores or restaurants, they will need to be processed according to local or state health codes. You will need to contact your local or state meat inspection agency for rules and regulations.

Meat

If you are slaughtering rabbits for home use, there are two ways to kill the rabbit. The neck can be dislocated by firmly grasping the hind legs and head. Then it is stretched to full length, and with a hard, sharp pull, the head is bent backward. This dislocates the neck. The other way to butcher the rabbit is to stun it with a hard blow behind the ears with a blunt object, like a stout stick or hammer.

Using a rope attached to one of the hind legs, hang the rabbit with the head down. Use a sharp knife to remove the head and allow the blood to drain from the carcass. The forefeet should next be removed right at the joint. Use the knife to cut the skin around the hock joint. Make a cut down the legs toward the tail and peel the hide down to the tail. Remove the tail and pull the skin down the rest of the body. Then, set the skin aside. Wash the knife to remove any blood clots or fur.

Next, make a cut starting near the anus and down the abdomen to the sternum. Cut through the entire abdominal muscle, but make sure you do not cut too deep and cut into the intestinal tract. You want to avoid this to keep from contaminating the meat with fecal material. Remove the intestinal tract and lungs; discard into the garbage. The heart, kidney, and liver can be removed and saved if desired. Once the abdominal contents are removed, take the rabbit off the rope and cut off the hind feet at the hock. The carcass should be washed with clean, running water to remove fur, blood clots, and other debris. The carcass should then be placed in sturdy, freezer bags and stored at refrigerator temperatures (35–40°F), or placed in the freezer if the meat is not consumed within two days.

Pelts

After removal from the body, the pelts should be processed while they are still warm and pliable. If there is any body fat present on the freshly skinned pelt, remove it by scraping with a sharp knife blade. The pelt should then be fitted around pelt shapers. These will expand the pelt to full length without stretching the pelts out of shape. Shapers can be made using sturdy wire, and the pelt can be fastened to the shaper with clothespins. The pelts on the shapers should be hung in a drying area but not in direct sunlight. After they are dried, they can then be removed from the shaper. The pelts are now ready for selling to fur dealers or for tanning.

How to Butcher a Sheep, Goat, Pig, or Steer

Butchering a larger animal will take some preparation and assistance. Many people prefer to have a local butcher shop do the job, as it is not an easy task. But if you prefer to butcher the animal for your own use, it is possible to perform the task at home. Large animals should be butchered when the outside daytime temperature is 40°F or cooler. This temperature is ideal refrigerator temperature and will allow the carcass to cool to prevent spoilage. Sheep and goats are usually butchered when they are fewer than 9 months old. Pigs generally are butchered when they weigh around 225 pounds. Cattle can be butchered as veal calves (around 2 to 3 months of age) or any time after this age.

The animal to be butchered should be removed from its herd mates and killed out of sight and hearing of the rest of the herd to keep from upsetting the other animals. Having a front-end load tractor will help you hang the animal so its blood can drain from the body. A pulley system consisting of a rope and block and tackle can also be used. Lead or drive the animal close to the area where you plan to hang the animal. You should also have a source of clean, running water in place near the butchering area.

Goats should be shot in the back of the head, while other animals are shot in the head at a point mid-way between the eyes. As soon as the animal is shot, sturdy ropes or chains should be placed on its rear legs, and it should be hung upside down. The jugular vein and carotid artery on the side of the throat should be slit to allow the blood to drain. The testicles on an uncastrated male animal should be removed next by cutting the attachments against the body. Following, the head of the animal should be removed. Goat or sheep heads can be removed by cutting around the neck with a knife and then severing the tendons and ligaments holding the head to the neck. Use a meat saw to sever the spine from the head in a pig or cow. Remove the front feet by cutting through the first joint on the leg.

The hide or skin will be removed next. A pointed knife should be used to make a circular cut in the hide around the rear legs. From each leg, make a cut through the hide and down the leg to the body. Join these cuts at the midline of the pelvis and extend the cut through the hide all the way down the abdomen to the neck. Skin the hide away from the body by removing the hide at the rear legs and working your way down the body. Pulling the loose skin as you make your cut will help peel the hide away.

After the skin has been removed, you will begin to remove the intestines. The tail should be removed in cattle at this point by severing the tail at the junction between it and the body. Use a pointed knife to cut around the anus to free the end of the colon from the attachment to the body. Give it a slight yank to completely free it, then tie it closed with a piece of clean string or twine. Use your knife to make a cut into the lower abdomen, being very careful not to puncture any internal organs. Extend the incision to the tip of the breastbone. Remove the penis in male animals at this point. Use a tub or a wheelbarrow to catch the intestines. Cut through the fat and tissue attachment holding the intestines inside the abdomen. Pull the anus out through the abdomen and gently, yet firmly, pull the intestines and bladder from the body. You can save the liver and kidneys at this point for your use if you desire. Once the intestines are out, you will need to sever the esophagus. This is the tube that runs from the mouth to the stomach. Try to cut it as far away from where it enters the stomach as possible. Once this is cut, the intestines should now be out of the carcass and in your container.

Next, cut through the diaphragm to remove the heart and lungs. Cut through the tissues attaching heart and lungs (the pluck) to the body and sever the windpipe at the top of the lungs. The heart can be saved, while the lung and windpipe are usually discarded along with the intestines. You will need to remove the rest of the windpipe by cutting through the neck to remove this structure. Once the internal organs are removed, wash the entire carcass inside and out with water, preferably from a running hose, to remove blood, hair, and debris. Allow the water to drain, then cover the carcass loosely with clean plastic.

Pig carcasses should hang overnight to chill the meat, then it will be ready to be cut into pieces. The carcasses of other animals should hang for a week (or more) in order to age the meat, which makes it more tender. Carcasses should only be allowed to hang outside if the temperature remains between 25 and 40°F — this is why it is best to butcher animals during the winter. If the temperature does not remain between this range, you will need to cut up the meat and freeze, or have an alternative refrigeration means available, such as a refrigerator at a local butcher shop.

A FINAL WORD

As much as it is rewarding, there will be times of frustration. Equipment may fail, animals may die, and predators may help themselves to your livestock. By paying careful attention to the material presented in this book and reading the case studies of people who have been there and done it, you will have the best chance of minimizing these negative factors. Careful planning and research can prevent many problems.

Like many projects, the best way to learn is by doing. If you are hesitant to have your own livestock at first, contact others in your area who are raising the species you are interested in and offer to help them out. But do not put off having your own little flock or herd for too long. As long as you have the space, necessary buildings, and enough finances, start out with a few birds or animals. You never know if a small project may eventually bloom into a sizeable income source.

No matter what your ultimate purpose is for raising livestock, remember to enjoy the process. Farming is hard work, but the benefits from the work are great: fresh air, physical work, and something new to be learned each day. Spend time with your animals; you can learn a lot by just observing and interacting with them.

One final important bit of advice: Remember to pass on what you know to a future small farmer. Teaching others is also a great way of reinforcing what you know. By being honest about the joys and pitfalls of farming, you can mentor others about the wonderful world of small-scale farming.

APPENDIX A

How to Make Butter

Making butter is a fairly straightforward process. You will need 1 to 1 ½ quarts of cream and 1 teaspoon salt. The cream should be at least 24 hours old in order to churn well. Let it stand at room temperature for four to six hours to ripen. This will make the cream thicken, and it will slightly sour, which will give the butter a great taste. Then, cool the cream in the refrigerator before you begin to churn it.

Place the cream into a large electric-mixer bowl. Beat the cream at high speed until butter flecks appear in the mixing bowl. Then reduce the speed to low and beat until the butter starts to separate from the milk. You will want to watch and scrape the bowl sides down with a spatula to push the cream off the sides.

Pour off the buttermilk and replace the amount removed with cold water. Continue to run the mixer at slow speed. As butter continues to churn, pour off the water and replace with an equal amount of cold water. Add the salt with this water. When it appears that the butter has formed into a ball in the mixer beaters, stop the mixer. Scrape the butter off the beaters and use the spatula to press the butter against the bowl's side to remove all the water. Place the butter into a container with a tight-fitting lid and store in refrigerator. After a few hours of work, you will have butter. One quart of cream will yield approximately one pound of butter.

How to Make Cheese

Cheese can be made from milk from goats, cows, and even sheep. Most dairy goats and dairy cows give more milk than can be used for drinking or cooking purposes. Making this excess into cheese is a fairly easy process, and most everyday kitchens will have the equipment necessary to make cheese. The main ingredients of cheese are fresh milk, a starter culture or acid, and rennet.

Simply put, making cheese involves removing the water from milk and congealing the solids left behind into a curd. This is done by one of two means: adding an acid directly to the milk or using bacteria to create the acid. The bacterial method is the preferred method, as it adds flavor to the finished cheese. Soft cheeses are cheeses in which less water is removed. Hard cheeses have more water removed and are generally aged longer than a soft cheese.

You will first want to pasteurize your milk if you are using it directly from the animal. This can be done by placing the milk in a double boiler and heating the milk to 161°F to kill any bacteria present in the milk. You will need to stir and carefully monitor the milk so it does not scorch. After the milk reaches the desired temperature, remove the top pan and place it in an ice water bath to cool the milk. A starter, or bacteria culture, is added next to the cooled milk. Many different types of starters are available depending upon the type of cheese you wish to make. These are readily available online or through specialty supply stores. The bacteria in the starter consume the milk sugar (lactose) and produce lactic acid. This acid then turns the milk solids into a curd. Rennet is then added — this enzyme comes from an animal or vegetable source and makes the curd coagulate.

After the rennet is added, the curd is allowed to sit for a few hours to gel. Then the curd is "cut" with a blade to allow the whey to rise to the top. The whey is then poured off, and the curd is mixed and heated, bringing more whey out of the curd. This extra whey is again poured off, and the curd is salted and placed in a cheesecloth or press. The cheese is then allowed to hang overnight (if in cheesecloth) or remain in the press to remove any remaining whey.

Most cheese starters will come with their own recipe. Follow the instructions that come with the starter for the best results. Depending on the type of cheese you are making, the cheese will be ready to eat from two days to months after making.

RESOURCES

General

Rodale Institute
www.rodaleinstitute.org

Land Stewardship Project
www.landstewardshipproject.org

Hobby Farms
www.hobbyfarms.com/livestock-and-pets/default.aspx

Supplies

Nasco
www.eNasco.com/farmandranch

Pipestone Veterinary Clinic
www.pipevet.com/pipevet/default.aspx

Pen Design

Free Chicken Coop Plans
www.freechickencoopplans.com

Dr. Temple Grandin: Livestock Behavior, Design of Facilities and Humane Slaughter
www.grandin.com

Iowa State University Cooperative Extension: Acreage Living
www.extension.iastate.edu/acreage/AL2000/al00pdf/aloct00.pdf

Poultry

The Poultry Site
www.thepoultrysite.com/diseaseinfo

Murray McMurray Hatchery
www.mcmurrayhatchery.com

Rabbits

American Rabbit Breeders Association
www.arba.net

Agricultural Alternatives: Rabbit Production
http://agalternatives.aers.psu.edu/Publications/rabbit.pdf

U.S. Department of Agriculture: Food Safety and Inspection Service
www.fsis.usda.gov/Fact_Sheets/Rabbit_from_Farm_to_Table/index.asp

Goats

American Dairy Goat Association
www.adga.org

American Boer Goat Association
www.abga.org

Sheep

American Sheep Industry Association
www.sheepusa.org

Minnesota West Community and Technical College:
Pipestone Lamb and Wool Program
www.pipestonesheep.com

Pigs

Maine Organic Farmers and Gardeners Association
www.mofga.org/Default.aspx?tabid=805

University of New Hampshire Cooperative Extension:
Raising Pigs at Home
http://extension.unh.edu/resources/resource/474/Raising_Pigs_at_Home_

Cattle

Northeast Organic Dairy Producers Alliance
www.nodpa.com

National Sustainable Agriculture Information Service:
Beef Farm Sustainability Checklist
http://attra.ncat.org/attra-pub/beefchek.html

Small Farm Marketing and Finance

U.S. Department of Agriculture National Agriculture Library:
Small Farm Funding Resources
www.nal.usda.gov/ric/ricpubs/small_farm_funding.htm

National Council of State Agricultural Finance Programs
www.stateagfinance.org/types.html

Cheese Making and Butchering Supplies

Leeners
www.leeners.com/cheese.html

Rodriguez Butcher Supply
www.homebutcher.com

F&T Fur Harvester's Trading Post
www.fntpost.com/Categories/Fur+Handling/Tanning/
Tanning+Kits+Supplies

The Home Processor
www.home-processor.com

BIBLIOGRAPHY

Damerow, Gail. *Barnyard in Your Backyard: A Beginner's Guide to Raising Chickens, Ducks, Geese, Rabbits, Goats, Sheep, and Cows.* Storey Publishing, 2002.

Guidry, Virginia Parker. *Rabbits: Complete Care Guide.* BowTie Press, 2002.

Hansen, Ann Larkin. *Beef Cattle: Keeping a Small-Scale Herd for Pleasure and Profit.* Hobby Farm Press, 2006.

Holderread, Dave. *Storey's Guide to Raising Ducks: Breeds, Care, Health.* Storey Publishing, 2000.

Kahn, Cynthia M. and Scott Line. *The Merck Veterinary Manual — 9th Edition.* Merck & Co., 2005.

Kellogg, Kathy and Bob. *Raising Pigs Successfully.* Williamson Publishing Company, 1985.

Tumey, Dianne. *Facts on Raising Gamebirds — 3rd Edition.* 1993.

Simmons, Paula and Carol Ekarius. *Storey's Guide to Raising Sheep: Breeds, Care, Facilities.* Storey Publishing, 2000.

Weaver, Sue. *Goats: Small-Scale Herding for Pleasure and Profit.* Hobby Farm Press, 2006.

AUTHOR BIO

Dr. Melissa Nelson is a graduate of the University Of
Minnesota — College Of Veterinary Medicine. She
currently resides on a beef cattle farm near Ortonville, Minn.

INDEX